COLOMBIA

BY PEG LOPATA

LUCENT BOOKS

An imprint of Thomson Gale, a part of The Thomson Corporation

Detroit • New York • San Francisco • San Diego • New Haven, Conn. • Waterville, Maine • London • Munich

Thanks to Jennifer and Agustín Diaz, Elsa Borraro, Andres Garay,
Fernando Cardona, and Nancy Ramirez Botello, who so kindly shared
Colombia with me. Also, thanks to my family of great readers,
Paul, Gabe, and Hillary.

LIBRARY OF CONGRESS CATALOGING-IN-PUBLICATION DATA

Lopata, Peg, 1958–
  Colombia / by Peg Lopata.
    p. cm. — (Modern nations of the world)
  Includes bibliographical references and index.
  ISBN 1-59018-110-7 (hard cover : alk. paper)
  1. Colombia--Juvenile literature. I. Title. II. Series.
F2258.5.L66 2004
986.1—dc22

                                                    2004010556

Printed in the United States of America

CONTENTS

INTRODUCTION

TURMOIL IN A LAND OF BEAUTY

Colombia is a land of many assets. It has many natural resources, such as oil, gold, silver, emeralds, platinum, and coal. Colombia also possesses an astounding array of scenic wonders. Yet these vast resources are scattered throughout a difficult terrain—mountains, impenetrable swamps, and deserts—that has long been an obstacle to national unity. The landscape has fragmented the country into rival families, disconnected regions, separate cultures, and limited trade. This lack of national unity has, over time, created many problems that have yet to be overcome, such as a decades-long war, high unemployment, poverty, and unchecked criminal activities. Outsiders do not easily understand the underlying reasons for these problems. In fact, according to David Bushnell, an American historian, "Colombia is the least studied and perhaps the least understood (by outsiders) of all the countries in Latin America."[1]

A LEGACY OF INEQUALITY AND VIOLENCE

Although Colombia's resources are abundant, Colombia has not developed all of its many resources for the common good of its people. Too often, only a few enjoy the profits of these plentiful resources. For instance, the best land for growing Colombia's most profitable crop, coffee, has been held for centuries by a small number of landowners. The thousands of peasants who have worked the land rarely have reaped the benefits of their hard work. This type of inequitable distribution of wealth, which for much of Colombia's history came from the land, is a serious problem in Colombia.

Colombia's largest problem, however, is its long history of political instability. Lasting national unity has yet to be achieved, even though the country has been a democracy for most of its years since independence. When the country established two dominant parties, Colombians fiercely aligned themselves to one party or the other. These divisions have led to widespread violence and corruption throughout Colombia.

For most of the modern era, liberals and conservatives have typically been the warring parties in Colombia's conflicts, despite the fact that their differences to an outsider—and some Colombians—might seem minor. In one of Colombia's most

Colombians mourn a celebrity killed by armed gunmen. Widespread violence resulting from political instability remains Colombia's most pressing problem.

famous novels, by Nobel Prize–winning writer Gabriel García Márquez, one of his characters exclaims, "The only difference today between Liberals and Conservatives is that the Liberals go to mass at five o'clock and the Conservatives at eight."[2] Although differences between the parties may seem slight, warring between Colombians became constant and commonplace. The country is embroiled in a civil war that continues with no end in sight.

OBSTACLES TO PEACE AND PROSPERITY

In addition to war, Colombia faces poverty, high unemployment, and an entrenched illegal drug trade. Because these problems have continued for so long, Colombians tend to consider their government institutions ineffective or corrupt. For example, the government has done little to ensure that Colombians have economic security and earn a living wage. Colombians have therefore not supported and have even rebelled against their government because it does not truly seem to serve the people.

Although this nation has never had a high standard of living, most recently Colombia has been coping with a serious economic decline that began in 1996. Since then more than a million Colombians, including many of Colombia's most educated citizens, have left their country to find opportunities elsewhere. In addition, widespread poverty and high unemployment have led some people to take drastic measures to survive. Some farmers turn to growing coca, despite the dangers of growing an illegal crop, just to make enough money to feed their families. Disgruntled young men join the well-established guerrilla forces or paramilitary armies—which fund their operations

Poverty and lack of opportunity drive many young Colombian men to join insurgent guerrilla groups that provide them with food and wages.

through the illegal drug industry—for a meal and a paycheck. Therefore the problems of unemployment and poverty fuel the ongoing war and illegal drug trade, which significantly drain the country of its revenues and threaten the safety of its people.

Another factor that continues to be an obstacle to prosperity and peace in Colombia is the inequitable judicial system. In Colombia the rule of law seems not to apply to those that are well connected or wealthy. For example, Colombia granted the country's most notorious criminal, Pablo Escobar, the right to build his own prison—which was in fact a luxurious home—as a last resort to getting this murderous drug dealer off the streets. This kind of favoritism has undermined the legitimacy of the legal system, thereby encouraging lawlessness.

OVERCOMING THE OBSTACLES

Colombia is struggling with many significant challenges but has engaged the support of a powerful ally, the United States, to combat one of its major problems: the illegal drug trade in cocaine. In fact, Colombia is the third largest recipient of financial aid from the United States, which provided over $1.7 billion in aid between 2000 and 2003. With such help, Colombia has the potential to become a prominent force in the Americas. The future might prove peaceful and prosperous for Colombia if it can improve in four critical areas: First, Colombia's leaders need to develop a political process that involves those who do not already hold political power; second, the economic system must distribute the nation's wealth more equitably; third, all Colombians must have access to economic opportunity; and finally, the government must improve its judicial system so that it provides true justice—the bedrock of a democracy—for all Colombians.

LAND OF MANY TREASURES

Colombia, a country about twice the size of Texas, is a land of dramatic contrasts, from fertile river valleys to snow-capped mountain peaks to sandy coasts. The country's great geographical diversity has created a nation defined by its regions instead of its thirty-two political divisions, called departments. Each region has its own customs, such as favorite music and legends. In the town of Mompós, for example, the men are nicknamed *los hombres caimánes* or "alligator-men" for this region's legend of a man who turns into an alligator when he goes into the Magdalena River.

Throughout Colombia's history each region has developed differently. For example, each area has a different climate that allows the people to grow a great diversity of foods. In this way, each area has been largely self-sufficient, and little commerce developed between regions. Distinct, original culture and customs arose from region to region. Although modern communications and air transportation now allow for greater national unity, each region has retained its own unique qualities.

THE GUAJIRA PENINSULA

Colombia's most northern mainland point is the Guajira Peninsula, a desert scrubland of 7,750 square miles jutting out into the Caribbean Sea. Like the American West, this area has been sparsely settled for most of its history because of its inhospitable hot climate, barren soil, and lack of water. The peninsula receives an average annual rainfall of less than ten inches, about the same as Tucson, Arizona. Also like the old American West, this area was and is still known for its lawlessness. With few government officials living here and law enforcement negligible, this great expanse of remote territory is a haven for those seeking to live outside the law.

Although the peninsula served as the landing point for the first Spanish explorers in 1499, the area was so remote and inhospitable that the Europeans were unable to conquer the people living here. Thus, indigenous peoples' descendants, the Wayuu of Guajira, many of whom work in the area's salt and coal mines, still survive here today. The Guajira Peninsula has little water, but it does have an abundant supply of salt and coal. In fact, the world's largest aboveground coal mine, El Correjón, which accounts for 65 percent of Colombia's coal production, is found here.

THE CARIBBEAN COASTAL REGION

West of the Guajira Peninsula is the Caribbean coastal region, which includes a lovely shoreline with beaches and quaint colonial towns and cities. The city of Cartagena, a former slave-trading center and once South America's most well-fortified city, is found here. Twenty-one percent of Colombia's population lives in this inland region and along the coast, making this area the nation's second most populated area. Most of the people living here are mulattoes, mixed race descendants of the Spaniards and African slaves. Inland from the coast are banana, cotton, and sugarcane plantations; cattle ranches; oil-rich plains; swamps; streams; and shallow lakes.

This region is home to many indigenous, or original, peoples. The descendants of a native people called Carib, the Motilón, still live here. They reside in the most isolated heights of the nearby mountain range, the Sierra Nevada de Santa Marta. Other natives, such as the Tayrona, also live in the mountains and live by farming and raising livestock. The Tayrona region is known as El Infierno or "Hell" because much of the area is covered with dense forests, thick swamps, and few roads and cannot be penetrated. The area is also famous for the Tayrona's ancient "lost city," La Ciudad Perdida, a major archaeological site discovered in 1975 by Julio César Sepúlveda.

The coastal region's ports have always connected this region to the outside world, especially the nearby Caribbean islands. Like the Caribbean islands, the Colombian coast is a favorite vacation spot due to its year-round warm weather. One major tourist attraction in the area is the Sierra Nevada de Santa Marta range, which includes Colombia's highest peak, Cristóbal Colón, at 18,947 feet. Off the coast is one of the world's largest coastal reef zones and a string of islands. One of

ZIPAQUIRA, OR SALT CATHEDRAL

About an hour's drive north from Bogotá is the Salt Cathedral, or Zipaquira, considered the eighth wonder of the world. Located 656 feet belowground is a 91,375-square-foot cathedral carved out of salt by numerous sculptors and artisans. The Salt Cathedral was opened in 1995. Visitors are encouraged to scrape the walls and lick their fingers to prove to themselves that the beautiful sculptures, statues, and religious symbols seen here are truly made of salt.

In one section of the cathedral there are statues representing symbols of the Catholic religion. Another section contains a brilliant white cross some fifty-two feet high and thirty-three feet wide carved out of an area of the wall, which is deep black due to impurities in the unrefined salt. The effect, in the words of author Marc Lessard in his book *Colombia,* "is miraculous, as the cross seems to be floating in the heavens."

The central gallery contains a marble sculpture by Carlos Enrique Rodríguez Arango called *The Creation of the World,* inspired by a scene from Michelangelo's paintings in the Sistine Chapel. There are also statues representing the Holy Family and Virgin Mary, both important symbols of the Catholic faith. The Salt Cathedral is a monumental testament to the deep faith of the Colombian people.

Visitors pray before the massive cross carved out of a wall in Zipaquira's subterranean cathedral.

The isolated heights of the Sierra Nevada de Santa Marta mountain range are home to many of Colombia's indigenous peoples.

these, San Andrés Island, supposedly has a buried cache of stolen gold taken from the Spanish by the famous sea pirate Henry Morgan.

THE PACIFIC COASTAL REGION

South of the Caribbean coastal region is a sparsely populated region bordered by the Pacific Ocean on the west and the Andean mountains to the east. Colombia's Pacific coast is 806 miles long with surrounding lowlands of numerous rivers, dense tropical forests, lagoons, thick swamps, and low-lying hills. In this hot climate zone some areas, especially those in the Chocó department, receive rainfall nearly every day, giving this region an average of over four hundred inches of rain a year. Numerous bird species are native to this region and several endangered mammals live here as well, such as the bush dog, a small, terrier-like wild dog that mainly eats rodents. The area is also home to giant anteaters as well as the Central American tapir, which is similar to a rhinoceros.

In the northernmost area of this region is the Atrato Swamp, which borders Panama. It is a deep, thick swamp teeming with wildlife. This swamp is so impenetrable that it has essentially kept Colombia from physically connecting to Central America. The Atrato Swamp interrupts a ten-thousand-mile-long road, the Pan-American Highway, which was supposed to run unbroken from northern Mexico to Argentina. But just south of the Panama border, in Colombia, the road is impassable except with four-wheel-drive vehicles. During the rainy season, it is only crossable by boat or on foot.

Today, the main connection to areas beyond the region is the Rio Atrato, the fastest flowing river in the world. The Rio Atrato flows northward to the Gulf of Urabá, connecting river settlements to major Caribbean ports. Because the people of this region can reach the Caribbean coast more easily than inland areas, they share Caribbean culture.

THE ANDEAN REGION

Eighty percent of Colombia's population lives in the Andean region's valleys and basins. Cutting through the region is the Andes mountain range, the longest high-mountain range in the world. This range extends some five thousand miles through seven countries in South America. The Colombian portion of the Andes is divided into three chains of mountains: the Cordillera Oriental, or eastern range; Cordillera Central, or central range; and Cordillera Occidental, or western range. These mountains cover about a third of the country. The highest peak, Nevado del Huila, is in the central range. This 18,865-foot-high mountain is in fact an old volcano. The country's most active volcanoes can also be found in the central range.

The Andean ridges have the most biodiverse high-altitude forests on the planet. The Muisca, a native group, named this mountainous region Cundinamarca or "heights where the condor dwells." Today, condors are still found in the higher regions. These vast tropical rain forests also have an average of 70 percent humidity year-round, creating ideal conditions for growing a great diversity of plants. Commercially useful trees such as mahogany, oak, walnut, cedar, pine, and balsam can be found here.

Despite being rich in resources, these mountains have limited communication and transportation throughout Colombia for most of its history. According to authors Frank Safford and Marco Palacios the Andes have "divided the country economically, politically and culturally." [3] Main routes across the three ranges through the middle of the nineteenth century, for example, could only be traveled by mule or horse and with great difficulty.

RESOURCES AND CROPS

The Andes are also rich in gold, silver, emeralds, salt, and two of today's most sought-after resources, coal and oil. Sugarcane and coffee are also plentiful. Most of the country's sugarcane comes from the western range while coffee is grown primarily in the central range, where thick deposits of volcanic ash have created a soil ideal for growing a great variety of plants. The Andean region has become more famous recently, however, for its illegal crops: coca and poppies, which when refined are sold as cocaine and heroin. Farming coca and poppies has increased because farmers can make more from those crops than they can selling coffee.

Key to favorable growing conditions throughout the Andean terrain are the numerous tributaries of its two main rivers, the Magdalena and the Cauca. The Magdalena flows between the central and eastern range and traverses nearly the entire country. Since pre-Columbian (before the arrival of Christopher Columbus to the Americas) times, the river provided a means of travel for all the peoples who have settled here, as well as passage inland from the sea for the explorers from Europe. The valley of the Cauca River has the richest farmland in the country, growing a great variety of crops, including sugarcane. Today, both the Cauca and Magdalena rivers create spectacular rapids and canyons and are the main source of energy for the country, supplying about 75 percent of Colombia's electric power.

BOGOTÁ AND MEDELLÍN

There are two major cities of the Andean region, Bogotá and Medellín. The capital, Bogotá, is the largest city in Colombia. It is about 8,660 feet above sea level, lying in a basin of the eastern range of the Andes. With temperatures averaging about fifty-eight degrees Fahrenheit year-round, the city is comfortably cool for its population of about 8.5 million people. Bogotá has been the center of this region since 200 B.C., when it was called Bacatá by the Muisca natives.

Bogotá is still considered the center of the country, and the nation's central political institutions are located here. The city is also one of Colombia's most productive cities. The city and its surrounding area account for nearly 23 percent of Colombia's gross national product, producing such commodities as food, chemicals, textiles, electrical equipment, plastics, and clothing. Yet despite this productivity and abundant natural resources, the nation's capital is also a city of beggars, shantytowns, and an alarmingly high crime rate, especially for murder and kidnapping.

The city of Medellín, also found in the Andean region, lies in the Aburra Valley at 4,900 feet between the western and central Andean ranges. It is sometimes called "the City of Eternal Spring" due to its temperate climate and moderate rainfall.

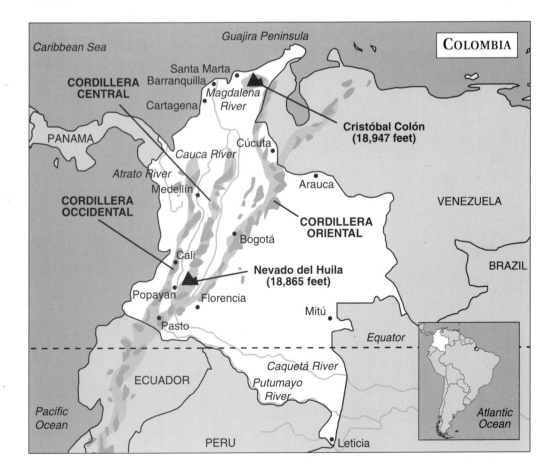

Medellín has a thriving textile and fashion industry and a world-class organ transplant program, and is the country's only city with a rapid transit system. Unfortunately, a huge influx of rural Colombians fleeing violence in the countryside has led to high unemployment and crime. Medellín is now one of the most violent cities in the world due to its illegal drug trade.

THE EASTERN REGION

Heading eastward from the Andean region is a vast grasslands region, or llanos, meaning "plains." These exceptionally flat plains account for nearly 63 percent of the landmass of the country, yet only about 2 percent of the population live here. There is little water, the climate is inhospitable, and there are few resources. This area's main industry is cattle ranching.

Southward from the llanos lies Colombia's rain forest, which accounts for about a third of Colombia's total landmass. This is a tropical region, covered in dense, primal forest. This area has few inhabitants, some of whom have lived apart from mainstream Colombian life for centuries.

Colombia's rain forest, like many rain forests around the world, is currently threatened by mining, agriculture, and ranching. Whereas these once impenetrable rain forests filled with rich resources were only used by Colombians with hand tools, global companies today utilize modern earth-moving and tree-cutting machinery that cuts huge swaths through the forests, creating access to minerals and forest products that are in great demand worldwide. Once roads are created in the rain forest, the land is cleared to grow crops and raise livestock.

The main town of the Amazon region is Leticia. It has a population of about thirty-three thousand and is situated near the border of Peru and Brazil. Here in Leticia and the surrounding area is a fifty-mile stretch along the Amazon River, the nation's only access to this river.

Although this region is only about the size of California, it accounts for more than 10 percent of the world's biodiversity. For example, in the Amazon zone, eight thousand different insects can be found in an area of less than twenty-five acres. In the Amazon department there are tigers, jaguars, monkeys, crocodiles, and snakes, including the anaconda, a snake as long as a school bus. The only freshwater dolphins on earth, some of which are a remarkable shade of pale pink, can be found here as well.

FLORA AND FAUNA

Because Colombia has such a stunning diversity of plant and animal life it is sometimes called the "world's gene bank." Colombia has the most species of birds, lizards, toads, and frogs—including the most poisonous frogs in the world, one

GAVIOTAS

The llanos are a barren savanna east of the Andes. Yet a thriving community of people and wildlife is growing there thanks to Paolo Lugari, a Colombian visionary, who, with the help of soil scientists and engineers, founded the community of Gaviotas. Lugari dreamed of creating a sustainable community on what is considered unlivable land. Today about two hundred people live there, working in the purified-water bottling plant, hospital, musical instrument and pine resins factories, or the medicinal plant research station.

The land's lack of natural resources provided many challenges that the Gaviotans overcame with resourcefulness and ingenuity. For example, the nearby muddy river could not supply clean water, so the Gaviotans built windmills to power water pumps to reach deep aquifers. They found clever ways to circulate water; for example, a seesaw at a local playground powers a water pump for a reservoir and a wading pool.

The Gaviotans also planted trees, particularly Caribbean pines, reforesting thirty-six thousand acres. Then, in what biologists call an unimaginable miracle, a tropical forest grew from seeds blown in, or brought by birds from the rain forest. Beneath the pines there are now some two hundred native species of plants. The Gaviotans of Colombia help to show how, with time and effort, ecological damage can be repaired and people can live where resources are in short supply.

of which has enough poison to kill several people. The country is also home to an abundance of insects; in fact, there are some three thousand species of mosquitoes found here. Colombia also has many unique mammals such as the white-footed tamarin, a type of primate (ape) about ten inches high. There is also the forest spiny pocket mouse, which is about five inches long with a tail almost twice as long. Also found here is the rare spectacled bear, which gets its name from the markings around its eyes. Colombia's two bodies of water, the Pacific Ocean and Caribbean Sea, contain shark, swordfish, tuna, shrimp, and many small, exotic fish that can be found in home aquariums around the world.

Colombia's climate encompasses almost all of the climates of the planet, thus producing an enormous variety of plants, most of which are found in the nation's tropical forests. Scientists consider these forests "the lungs of the earth" because they produce a great deal of oxygen, which is vital for the survival of all animal life. Over 130,000 plant species have been identified throughout Colombia. Colombia also has the largest number of orchid and palm species in the world. Some 20,000 of the plant species found here are unique to Colombia, such as the world's tallest palm, the Quidio palm, one of the country's national emblems. One curious plant, the *Victoria amazonica,* has leaves large and strong enough for a child to stand upon.

Within the borders of this country, from its remote snowy mountaintops to the crowded strips of sand, Colombia's geography has been both a curse and a blessing for the people who live here. The land provided well for the ancient peoples who lived here. Yet the treasures of their land—especially their gold—lured fortune-hunting outsiders. After those first outsiders laid their eyes on the riches of this most beautiful and difficult place, the land and its people would forever be changed.

2

LAND OF MANY CULTURES

For much of its history Colombia has been a collection of distinct regions with many different cultures. From preconquest through the colonial era and the early days as a republic, the people of Colombia have had strong pride in their native villages, towns, and cities. But that pride came at a price. Due to little or no national unity most of Colombia's history was fraught with conflicts and instability.

BEFORE EUROPEAN EXPLORATION

Before the arrival of Europeans, the land now called Colombia was sparsely settled by about twelve independent groups of peoples. There was no centralizing tribe, such as the Incas in Peru or the Aztecs in Mexico, to unify the people in one culture. Instead, the groups of Colombia developed widely different customs and cultures. Some were well organized, such as the approximately 1 million Muisca who lived in small farming villages throughout the Andean basins in central Colombia. Others, such as the Guahibo of the eastern plains, were nomadic, meaning they did not live in settled villages but moved from place to place following the resources they needed to survive.

Most of the settled people throughout these lands lived in small thatch-roofed homes with mud or wood sides. But some, such as the Sinú, who lived in northern Colombia, had more elaborate structures. They allegedly had a temple so large that it could hold one thousand people. The Muisca buildings were so impressive that the first Spaniards to arrive here nicknamed the area "valley of castles."

When they lived in settled communities, most of these groups grew a variety of crops such as cotton, corn, tomatoes, potatoes, cacao, and tobacco. Some had elaborate irrigation systems and terraced the mountainsides for farming. Many groups panned for gold in the rivers or dug it out of the earth and were known for their metalwork, especially items wrought in gold. They were also known for fine pottery and textiles.

These groups were constantly at war with each other. Believing that they would acquire their captives' strength and courage, some tribes ate the people they captured. According to Spanish chronicler Bernal Díaz del Castillo, "They [the native peoples] ate their prisoners right on the battlefield, stewed in pots with salt, peppers and tomatoes."[4]

EUROPEANS' SEARCH FOR GOLD

European explorers arrived in Colombia at the end of the sixteenth century in search of a new passage to the Asian continent. These adventurers were often accompanied by Christian clergy who came to convert native peoples, or "Indians," as they were erroneously named by the Europeans.

Many of Colombia's indigenous peoples were skilled metalworkers. Pictured is a gold pendant of the Sinú people, who lived in northern Colombia.

THE LEGEND OF EL DORADO

The most famous Colombian legend is based on a Muisca story and ritual. According to the Muisca, long before the arrival of the Spaniards, a huge meteor fell from the sky. The crater made by the meteor filled with water, forming a lagoon, called Laguna de Guatavita. Whenever the people celebrated a new leader, he was brought to the lagoon, anointed with oil, and then covered with gold dust. The people heaped great amounts of gold and emeralds on a beautiful raft decorated with precious gems and metals. Their new leader, accompanied by his chiefs, then set sail on the sacred lagoon. When the raft reached the center of the lagoon, the gilded leader and his chiefs threw all the riches into the water.

When the Spanish explorers heard this legend, they became obsessed with finding this lagoon, whose bottom they hoped would be covered with unimaginable treasures. They also wanted to find El Dorado, the gilded man. Many explorers died in search of the golden man and his kingdom of gold. The Laguna de Guatavita was excavated many times in search of emeralds and gold, but little was found. In 1965 the lagoon was proclaimed a national monument, putting an end to any further treasure hunting.

But the legend lives on. "El Dorado" came to mean a mythical place where the streets were paved with gold, the buildings were built of gold, and the people were adorned head to toe in gold. To this day, whenever someone is in search of a fabulous fortune, they are said to be seeking El Dorado.

The first European to arrive in what is now Colombia was Alonso de Ojeda. He landed on the Guajira Penisula on the Caribbean coast in 1499. In 1535 Gonzalo Jimenéz de Quesada, Nikolaus Federmann, and Sebastián de Belalcázar explored the country, each beginning separate expeditions from three different starting points: Peru, Venezuela, and Colombia. Some indigenous groups fought off these invaders quite successfully with weapons such as poisoned arrows. Others welcomed them, believing that they were the benevolent gods of their legends. Little did they know their people would be almost completely destroyed in the next one hundred years by these pale-skinned visitors.

Quesada, whose explorations began on the Caribbean coast, quickly noticed that the Indians there wore and used gold. To get rid of the explorers, the coastal natives reportedly told Quesada that the source of the gold could be found inland. Quesada and his men quickly went off on their treasure hunt. The other two explorers also came across native peoples adorned with gold and headed inland, where they too believed more gold could be found. Thus began one of the bloodiest and most horrific chapters of Colombian history. Wherever the explorers went, they stole the natives' food; enslaved them to carry their loads for their torturous travels through swamps, mountains, and deserts; and killed whoever did not cooperate. To survive, the explorers ate their dogs, horses, and even occasionally each other. As author John Hemming puts it, "The European adventurers were like a pack of hounds roaming the interior to pick up the scent of gold."[5]

The three groups of explorers were all headed in the same direction—to the land of the Muisca peoples. The first to arrive was Quesada. The Muisca were terrified by his horses. They had never seen a horse before. Believing him to be a member of the forest-dwelling Panches, a cannibal tribe that lived to their south, the Muisca offered him children to eat.

Quesada found his journey to the land of the Muisca well rewarded. They had an abundance of gold. The Muisca buried gold with their dead, wore gold armor and ornaments—and they even used sheets of gold to keep the rain off their buildings. Quesada and his men took whatever gold they could get their hands on. They frightened the peasants into submission with superior weaponry and cavalry. Many of the Muisca were then enslaved by Quesada and his men.

Eventually, the king of Spain divided up the lands that the explorers had traveled through among Quesada, Federmann, and Belalcázar. In 1564 the territory was incorporated by Spain into a viceroyalty called New Granada, which included most of present-day Colombia and Panama. The viceroyalty was ruled from Peru by the viceroy, a government official appointed by the king of Spain.

THE CONQUEST OF THE NATIVES

Although the territory was now officially ruled by Spain, few Spanish laws were followed, especially regarding the treatment of the indigenous peoples. The explorers ruled over them like ruthless dictators. On expeditions, they used the natives like pack mules, forcing them to carry supplies and the explorers themselves on chairs strapped to the natives' backs. They forced the natives to pay what was called a tribute which consisted of gold, goods, or food. When natives could not pay the tribute, they were forced into slavery. Some adult males were sent far from their homes to mine for gold. This grueling type of labor killed many people. The women were often raped and their children enslaved; their families were forced to become Christians.

Some of the indigenous peoples ran off; some stayed and became slaves. Others tried to rebel by fighting or destroying crops. Some tried to protect themselves through peaceful means. They would go to court, for example, to try to gain legal rights to own property or have the freedom to work as they wanted. But ultimately, the natives could not survive the inhuman cruelties of the Europeans. As summarized by author Marc Lessard, "The natives were systematically cheated, robbed, violated and ultimately decimated."[6]

THE BIRTH OF A COLONY

While the explorers roamed South America, their rulers in Spain, especially church authorities, began to believe enslaving the Indians was morally wrong. The Spanish government ultimately issued decrees called the New Laws to control the onslaught against the indigenous peoples of the newly conquered land. The decrees were ineffective, however, because lawlessness was rampant throughout these territories and little could be done to control the situation. There were few authorities to watch over the explorers, and fewer still who had any power to stop them from enslaving and stealing from the indigenous peoples. Sentiment against colonization continued in Spain, and in 1550 a royal decree ordered the suspension of all conquests, expeditions, and exploration. The ban, however, lasted for only ten years, after which conquests resumed as more and more explorers arrived in New Granada in search of gold.

Settlements grew where there was gold or silver to be mined and natives to be converted to Christianity. Both settlers and indigenous people lived in huts made of reeds sealed with dried mud and later in huts of pressed earth and thatched roofs. Some settlements grew quite large. By 1570 Bogotá had about six hundred Spanish men and forty thousand male Indians. As populations grew, monasteries and

convents were built. The church became a vital element of colonial life by running schools and maintaining some aspects of social order, such as enforcing rules governing marriage, ensuring parents took care of their children, conducting rites of passage, and settling village and familial disputes.

A NEW CULTURE ARISES

As the colony grew, the culture became less and less indigenous and more and more Spanish and Christian. New generations of

Throughout the sixteenth century, Spanish missionaries in Colombia built churches like this one in the town of Cauca to help their effort to Christianize the indigenous peoples.

American Spaniards were born. A class system eventually arose based on skin color, family origins, and occupation. Those with a purely Spanish heritage but born in the colony were called creoles; those who were part Spanish and part Indian were called mestizos. Mestizos and indigenous peoples were at the bottom of the social order—they had little to no power over their lives and no say in how the country was run.

NICARAGUA
COSTA RICA
PANAMA
VENEZUELA
GUYANA
SURINAME
FRENCH GUIANA
COLOMBIA
ECUADOR
PERU
BRAZIL
BOLIVIA
PARAGUAY
CHILE
South Pacific Ocean
South Atlantic Ocean
ARGENTINA
URUGUAY

SPANISH-CONTROLLED COLONIES

PRESENT-DAY POLITICAL BOUNDARIES

COLONIES IN SOUTH AMERICA AT THE HEIGHT OF THE SPANISH EMPIRE

Creoles were in the middle—they had some power. The colonists who were born in Spain had the highest status of all.

As the colony grew, indigenous people were slowly disappearing due to assimilation, overwork, famine, and European diseases. Their culture was also phased out as they were prohibited from freely practicing their religion and wearing their traditional clothing. Along the Caribbean coast as much as 95 percent of the indigenous population was wiped out by the 1700s. To replace the dwindling Indian workforce, the Spaniards shipped in tens of thousands of African slaves during the 1700s, thus adding yet another culture to the land. African slaves eventually outnumbered the indigenous population. Although slavery was not officially abolished until 1852, the practice waned by the 1700s, and the slaves joined the population as free people. The former slaves, like the remaining indigenous peoples, were at the bottom of the social ladder.

Meanwhile, the colony expanded its borders to include what is now Colombia, Ecuador, Panama, most of Venezuela, and Trinidad and Margarita, two Caribbean islands off the coast of Venezuela. Although this entire territory was under common rule by Spain, the country was still not unified. The culture retained the imprint of the many kinds of people living here. The class system, the variety of people present on the land, and the unpassable terrain all fostered divisions in the region. Consequently, people grew strongly loyal to their classes, their origins, and their own particular regions instead of to the nation as a whole. Moreover, although the colony was still controlled by Spain, Europe seemed very far away indeed. Conflicts between groups and also between the colonists and the Spanish crown were inevitable.

SPAIN LOSES CONTROL

The first major conflict began with the rise of a well-to-do and educated creole class wanting more political power. They particularly resented that most of the colonial government was run by people who had been born in Spain. Complicating things further was the division of the colony into three main centers of control. Bogotá held political power, the west held economic power, and Cartagena controlled commerce with the outside world. As each vied for power, the colony became fragmented and disorganized.

Spain sought to gain better control over its colony throughout the 1700s by increasing military forces, hiring more government officials—most of whom were Spaniards—and severely enforcing tax collection. To control the native population, who had scattered to dispersed communities, the Spanish rulers relocated them into Spanish-controlled towns to live under the authority of a Spaniard. The officials, both governmental and church clergy, wanted to keep a close eye on the native population to make sure they were following Christian practices, obeying colonial rules, and not reverting to their indigenous way of life. As authors Frank Safford and Marcos Palacios say, "Officials and churchmen wanted these people to live within earshot of the church bell." [7]

But the Spaniards were fighting a losing battle. They could not control the colonists nor the indigenous peoples. It was nearly impossible to govern isolated cities, towns, and villages that were scattered throughout a vast land. According to Safford and Palacios, "The viceroy [the Spanish-appointed official in Peru] could not possibly govern this far-flung expanse. He had very little contact with Ecuador and had almost no idea what was going on in Venezuela." [8]

FIRST CHALLENGES TO COLONIAL RULE

The creoles were the first to directly challenge Spanish authority. As descendants of the first explorers, they saw themselves as "owners" of this land and wanted to be appointed to important positions in the government. They were only allowed to buy lower-level government positions, so if they could afford it, some creoles did become involved in running the local government. But these marginal positions were not enough. Creoles were still not in control of the colony. By the mid–eighteenth century, the creoles' resentment over their lack of power was about to boil over in open revolt.

Other groups resented Spanish rule as well. For example, the mestizos had their own particular grievances. They were not allowed to attend the universities or hold public positions at all. Like the creoles, they also resented being dominated by European-born Spaniards. In addition, as they felt no special allegiance to Spain, they resented paying taxes that supported Spain's wars elsewhere in the world. Indeed, almost everyone in New Granada despised the high taxes on practically all goods. As described by authors Jesús María Henao and Gerardo Arrubla, "Even eggs and thread were taxed. . . . So many articles were taxed . . . the list was a yard and a quarter long."[9] The people also resented the government's monopoly on tobacco and liquor. They wanted to trade freely in these two valuable goods, but only a chosen few were allowed to sell these products.

Adding fuel to fire was news of revolutions in North America and France. Around the world, people rebelled against religious doctrines and demanded their share of power in economic and political affairs. The colonists were inspired by new ideas about governance, especially the rights of individuals. Books and treatises about these radical ideas were imported from Europe and circulated among the educated peoples in New Granada.

REBELLION WITH LOYALTY

Revolt eventually spread to New Granada. Throughout the 1760s there were substantial riots throughout the colony. The first significant rebellion, the Comunero Revolt, occurred in 1781. The protestors demanded a repeal of new taxes and changes in trade laws. They also demanded that creoles be appointed to higher-level positions in the government. But these first rebels did not yet seek complete independence from colonial rule. They just wanted greater say in economic affairs that directly affected their lives. While the colonists opposed trade restrictions and fought for more rights, they always remained loyal to their Spanish king. For example, when French emperor Napoléon invaded Spain and put his brother on the Spanish throne in 1808, the colonists refused to recognize the new monarch and declared war on Napoléon in support of their king.

With the Spanish king in exile, the colonists sought to establish some form of self-rule, not in opposition to their motherland, but merely to maintain some order in governing the colony. Government

When French emperor Napoléon Bonaparte installed his brother Joseph (pictured) on the Spanish throne in 1808, the colonists of Colombia refused to recognize his sovereignty.

officials in Bogotá established a new, temporary ruling body. This supreme court was composed of elected officials—some creole, some Spanish—to ensure continued governance of New Granada. These officials requested that representatives be sent from the other provinces to serve on this court. Many provinces refused as they did not recognize the authority of Bogotá and wanted to rule themselves rather than submit to the supreme court's rule.

The lack of unity among the colonists proved fatal for the movement toward increased self-rule. The colonists' strong sense of regional loyalty was greater than their desire to unite. In addition, a split soon developed in this temporary New Granadan government. Although both wanted to remain subjects of the Spanish crown, on one side were the federalists, or those who wanted autonomous states, and on the other side were the centralists, who wanted a strong central government to govern one unified country. Without a strong centralized leadership to resolve this conflict, these two factions would spend decades fighting each other over this disagreement, keeping the country divided for many years to come.

Meanwhile, unrest continued throughout the country. Between 1809 and 1815 several cities rebelled against their rulers and demanded representation in the provisional government of Spain. Cartagena declared absolute independence from Spain on November 11, 1811. Other cities soon followed.

Although isolated cities declared their independence from Spain, the entire country of New Granada still failed to overthrow Spanish rule for several reasons. The church undermined popular support for the independence movement by telling the people that rebellion against the king was the same as rebelling against God. Further complicating matters were internal struggles among the leaders, which exhausted their resources and spirit. There was also continuing opposition to centralized control—allegiance to particular families and regions was still stronger than any unifying nationalist sentiment. Finally, the movement for independence was not widely supported by the peasants and the slaves who were promised land and freedom for their support of the crown.

COLONIAL RULE RETURNS

By 1816 New Granada was comprised of pockets of inhabitants scattered throughout the country that for the most part

Ferdinand VII, the king of Spain, installed a violently repressive regime in Colombia in order to maintain Spanish control of the colony.

ruled themselves. The colonial rulers were ineffective in maintaining order over the population. People were pulled apart in the quest for independence. Minor uprisings and unrest was common throughout the colony. Anarchy spread. To control the unrest the reinstalled king of Spain, Ferdinand VII, sent Spanish general Pablo Morillo to pacify the people. He granted pardons to those colonists who laid down their arms and swore loyalty to the Spanish crown. He granted freedom to slaves who joined his campaign. In 1815 his forces captured Cartagena. Morillo went on to reconquer New Granada by severe tactics. For example, he executed leaders of the independence movement, such as Camilo Torres, an eloquent patriot, and confiscated property of rebel colonists. He soon controlled the entire colony, which still included what is now Colombia, Ecuador, Panama, most of Venezuela, and two Caribbean islands off the coast of Venezuela, Trinidad and Margarita.

To further curtail any new attempts at rebellion, a violently repressive Spanish military regime was installed. Various tribunals to punish exiles and prisoners were established. Even priests who had supported the independence movement were severely punished. However, the newly installed regime's tactics for controlling the people ultimately failed. The cruelties

ANTONIO NARIÑO: PRECURSOR OF COLOMBIAN INDEPENDENCE

Antonio Nariño was one of Colombia's greatest patriots. He is called "the Precursor" because his work toward freeing Colombia from Spanish rule came before Colombia's widespread movement for independence. One of his first acts of rebellion against Spain came in 1793, when he translated and distributed *The Declaration of the Rights of Man* by the American patriot Thomas Paine.

When the viceroy of Bogotá heard that Nariño wanted Colombia to gain independence from Spain just as the Americans had attained independence from England, the authorities searched Nariño's home. When they found many forbidden books, he was arrested and sentenced to ten years in prison in Africa. En route to Africa, Nariño managed to jump ship in Spain and returned to his homeland disguised as a priest. He traveled throughout the country, listening to people's grievances against the government. Despite his disguise, he was soon recognized and sent to prison in Cartagena.

Nariño was released in 1803 but imprisoned again in 1809 for plotting to overthrow the government. He was freed at the end of 1810 and resumed his battle for an independent Colombia. He soon became the president of the province Cundinamarca. After two years of violent conflicts within the revolutionary movement, Nariño was captured by royalists and shipped off to prison in Spain in 1814.

In 1820 Nariño returned home to the newly independent Gran Colombia. He was welcomed by Simon Bolívar, who appointed him vice president. Because of a lifetime devoted to the liberation of Colombia, Nariño is known today as one of the precursors to independence.

used to control the people fueled further resentment against the crown, fostering the quest for independence among more and more people. In addition, when the new regime failed to fulfill promises made to the peasants and the slaves, such as land rights and freedom, they became eager to overthrow Spanish rule.

The first movement for independence from the years 1810 to 1816 was seen as a failure filled with mistakes and missteps; in fact, the independence movement was later called by Colombian historians *Patria Boba,* or "foolish fatherland." Yet during this time significant progress was made toward independence. For instance, July 20, 1810 (the day New Granada's first constitution was written), is celebrated today as Colombia's anniversary of the revolution even though formal independence was not achieved until 1819. The constitution is notable in that it demanded liberty for the individual and autonomy of the provinces of New Granada.

INDEPENDENCE IS WON

The next attempt at independence began in 1819, this time with a seasoned military leader, Venezuelan Simon Bolívar, leading the charge against the royalist forces stationed in Bogotá. Instead of disorganized pockets of rebellion, like that which occured previously, this time the rebel colonists had much greater widespread support among the masses. Bolívar and his forces won a number of military encounters. They defeated the Spanish royalists on the road to Bogotá near the Boyacá River on August 7, 1819, destroying the main Spanish army. They then marched unopposed into Bogotá, the heart of colonial rule.

Authors Jesús María Henao and Gerardo Arrubla describe the celebratory scene welcoming the patriots into Bogotá: "Bolívar was crowned with a laurel wreath. He put the wreath successively on the heads of [fellow patriots] and then threw it to the troops, saying 'Those liberators are the ones who deserve these laurels!'" [10] Bolívar came to be known as "el Libertador," or "the Liberator." Independence was won. With the main Spanish army defeated, Spain could no longer maintain rule throughout the country. Three hundred years of colonial rule came to an end.

In 1821 Venezuela and New Granada were officially joined as one independent nation called Gran Colombia, which included present-day Colombia, Venezuela, and Panama. Bolívar became president and Francisco de Paula Santander, a fellow patriot, vice president. Ecuador was added to Gran Colombia when it achieved liberation from Spain in 1822. However, the colonists' victory over their colonial ruler did not yet create a nation. The Spaniards did not leave behind stable political institutions or experienced legislators, making the new nation shaky in its infrastructure. Furthermore, the country's leaders were already divided between centralists and federalists. The centralists still wanted a strong, centralized government, whereas the federalists wanted a nation of autonomous states with little centralized control.

Another major obstacle to building a nation was division among the people. In Bogotá there was a sense of what independence meant, and the people celebrated their liberation. Elsewhere, however, the people knew or cared little about these political changes. The peasants, who comprised the vast majority of the population, continued to obey the landowners who functioned as the authority, providing them with, although meager, a livelihood and protection from enemies. To the peasants, this arrangement continued regardless of who ran the country. Furthermore, each province had its own capital, and people were for the most part loyal to their regional leaders, not the leaders in Bogotá. The lack of national unity led to many decades of upheaval and conflict in Colombia.

A DIVIDED NATION

After achieving independence in 1819, Gran Colombia began its long road toward building a democracy. As in many Latin American countries, nation building did not come easy, and many violent conflicts marred the nineteenth and twentieth centuries. Colombians continued to be more loyal to their families, landowners, the church, and regions rather than their newly formed country.

ORGANIZING THE NEW REPUBLIC

To begin building a nation, the leaders of the revolution met in what was called the Cúcata Congress in 1821 to organize a government and write a constitution for Gran Colombia, which by this time encompassed parts of present-day Venezuela and Ecuador and all of present-day Colombia and Panama. Attempts to organize the newly independent nation soon failed, however, as its early leaders split into rival factions over many issues, such as what kind of government to have and what role the Roman Catholic Church should play in it. They also could not agree on economic issues, such as taxation and rules about trade.

While the members of congress tried to organize a government, the country had few authorities to maintain control and gradually slipped into chaos. Taxes were not collected, government officials were not paid, and most dangerously, laws were not respected. Although the fight for liberty had freed the country from Spanish rule, the people did not pull together as one unified nation. Regionally based cultural differences and a lack of central authority allowed small conflicts to fester. In the next few years numerous violent outbreaks were pulling the fragile new country apart.

To control the unrest, government leaders met in 1828 and tried to rewrite the constitution. Unfortunately, again they fought among themselves and made no agreements. Francisco de Paula Santander, the vice president, supported a federalist, or decentralized, form of government, meaning each

The first president of Gran Colombia, Simon Bolívar, believed the country needed a strong centralized government.

region should maintain primary control over itself and choose its own leader. The president, Simon Bolívar, believed the country would be better managed with a strong centralized government that put standards in place for each region, such as requiring all regions to have public education for all children. He also believed a governing body that would appoint leaders of the separate regions should be located in the country's capital.

Leaders also continued to argue over what role the church should have in governing the country. They all agreed the country would be a Catholic nation—indeed, the constitution did not grant freedom of religion. There was strong disagreement over how much the church should be involved in governing Gran Colombia, however. The centralists wanted the church to be involved in government affairs. The federalists, on the other hand, wanted a stronger separation between church and state.

Meanwhile, widespread unrest spread throughout the ungoverned country. To gain control, Bolívar censored the press and fired his vice president Santander. Yet chaos continued. By 1830 the financial affairs of Gran Colombia collapsed due to the political infighting and unrest. Foreign trade declined and the government was unable to collect revenue. Consequently, it could not run its own affairs, such as paying the military and other government employees.

Bolívar eventually became hopelessly discouraged and frustrated with the process of organizing his country and resigned in 1830. He felt that the men who fought for freedom from the Spanish had achieved nothing. Just a few months before he died he expressed this pointlessness when he wrote, "Those who have worked for the cause of Latin American freedom have plowed the sea."[11] Unable to withstand the pressure, in 1830 Gran Colombia split into three separate countries: New Granada (as Colombia was called decades earlier in the mid-1700s), Venezuela, and Ecuador.

Although politically the country was failing apart, the ordinary citizen was far removed from all this upheaval in political affairs. Despite liberation from Spain, a new constitution, and the transformation from Gran Colombia to New Granada, most of the people lived as they had done for hundreds of years: farming, raising livestock, or selling handicrafts. About 90 percent of the population lived in rural areas. They were extremely poor, but the abundant supply of potatoes, corn, and plantains (a type of banana) kept them from starving.

The social order remained unchanged as well. Workers continued to be subservient to landowners. For example, although not slaves, the peasants addressed their employers as "master." As author David Bushnell explains, "Democracy was not developing. In 1840, a visiting Frenchman recorded

A mural celebrates Simon Bolívar as the liberator of the Colombian people. In actuality, however, the lives of ordinary Colombians changed very little after independence was achieved.

his impressions. 'What is one to expect from a republic where every man calls "master" any individual whiter or dressed better than himself?'" [12] However, there were some social improvements. For instance, in 1852 slavery was abolished. And in 1853 a new constitution granted the right to vote to men, and provided for freedom of worship, separation of church and state, the legitimacy of civil marriages, and the legalization of divorce.

As the nineteenth century progressed, advancements in transportation and industry slowly improved the lives of New Granadans. For example, steamships now traveled on the Magdalena river, bringing much needed products, such as goods made of iron, to more remote areas. Guns, stoves, and sturdier building materials improved the lives of the peasants. In 1850 the country built its first railroad, connecting Colombia to the province of Panama. The railroad also linked the country to North America, expanding trade routes, which helped improve the economy. Many industries also had far fewer restrictions, so trade flowed more freely. For example, the government no longer controlled the tobacco industry, so anyone—not just government-approved farmers—was now allowed to participate in the lucrative market of growing and selling tobacco.

TWO PARTIES SPLIT THE NATION

Despite industrial and economic gains, New Granada continued to flounder primarily because of the ongoing struggles between the federalists, who eventually became the Liberal Party, and the centralists, who became the Conservative Party. Unable to agree on critical issues, the two parties split the country into fierce rival factions. As explained by author Marc Lessard, "The chasm between the parties grew deep and wide and while the two parties were preoccupied with their own quarrels, the provinces [of New Granada] became almost totally autonomous [self-governing]." [13] In fact, between 1863 and 1886 some forty different constitutions were written for the nine provinces, and the country was renamed twice. (The constitution of 1886 renamed the country the Republic of Colombia, as it is known today.) About fifty insurrections and nineteen civil wars during this time further ravaged the new nation.

The worst of the conflicts, known as the War of a Thousand Days, began in July 1899 when the Liberals revolted to unseat the Conservative government. The war lasted for one

COFFEE: COLOMBIA'S KING CROP

Coffee has long played an important role in the economy and development of Colombia. In the beginning of the nineteenth century, Jesuit priests brought coffee bushes to Colombia and discovered that the slopes of the Andes mountains were ideally suited for the cultivation of coffee. The bushes flourished, and export of coffee began in 1835. With the money earned from the coffee industry, roads, railroads, harbors, schools, and health clinics were built. The capital of the Antioquia department, Medellín, in the heart of the coffee-growing region, became the industrial capital of the country.

In 1927 a federation of coffee growers was established. The federation funded research for improving coffee, established standards of quality, and provided technical and financial assistance to coffee growers. By 1930 Colombia was the world's second leading coffee producer, a title the nation retains today. Coffee will no doubt continue to play a key role in the country's economy and lives of many Colombians.

thousand days and claimed the lives of some one hundred thousand men. Writes author Harvey Kline, "The soil of the fatherland was inundated with blood, thousands of Colombians died on the battle fields. . . . and the country found itself completely ruined."[14] After the War of a Thousand Days, which ended in 1902, the country was once again weak and unstable. Panama, one of the provinces, took advantage of the country's instability and sought liberation from Colombia. With the help of the United States, Panama seceded from Colombia in 1903.

The loss of Panama stung. But since Panama had always been a far-flung, culturally separate province, the loss actually helped what remained of Colombia to develop a national identity as its territory shrank to a more manageable size. Still, Colombia's leaders recognized that losing Panama might have been prevented if New Granada had been a more cohesive country. The leadership was now more determined than ever to rise above their internal squabbling and work together to build a stable nation.

STABILITY AND HARDSHIP IN THE TWENTIETH CENTURY

From 1904 to 1930 Colombia enjoyed a phase of stability in which power was peacefully shared between the two parties.

During this time period one president in particular, General Rafael Reyes, worked to unify the republic and restore the nation's economy. President Reyes encouraged foreign investment and improved the nation's transportation system. He encouraged exportation of petroleum and agricultural products such as bananas and especially coffee, which was quickly replacing gold as the country's main export.

Daily life remained difficult for many rural people, however. Food and medicine were at times scarce, and most Colombians were poor and uneducated. For example, by 1930 most Colombians could not read and the average life expectancy was thirty-four years. There was, as Alfonso López Pumarejo, president from 1934 to 1938, wrote, "a vast and miserable economic class that does not read, that does not write, that does not dress, that does not wear shoes, that barely eats, that remains . . . on the margins of national life." [15]

To address the problems of this "vast and miserable class" Pumarejo launched a program called the Revolution of the March that included many social reforms. For example, recognizing that many Colombians could neither read nor write but should be given the right to vote, Pumarejo eliminated the literacy requirement for voting. To ensure that peasants did not starve, he gave poor people more land. Pumarejo's administration also added constitutional amendments that helped to develop the country's economy, ensured the rights of labor union workers, and established some forms of public assistance. Due to these reforms, the economy improved and industry expanded; better transportation and communications systems unified the country.

However, by 1942 the country was yet again in decline, suffering from the effects of World War II. The war disrupted trade of the usual goods, increasing the prices for imported goods. All over the world, people bought fewer so-called luxuries, especially one particular luxury that greatly affected the economy of Colombia—coffee. Against this backdrop political tensions ran high, and street fighting and demonstrations erupted in Bogotá. A military coup attempted to overthrow Pumarejo, who resigned in 1945. But the political unrest that led to his resignation did not subside. His many reforms had indeed improved the lives of peasants but also left angry wealthy landowners, powerful businessmen, and church officials who were determined to undo what he had accomplished.

THE COLLAPSE OF DEMOCRACY

Beginning in 1946 Colombia's democratic system slowly started to collapse. The years of mistrust, hatred, and tensions that had existed between the parties returned and was compounded by widespread social frustration. Colombia finally erupted in civil war that began one of the bloodiest and ugliest periods in Colombian history. For the next decade Colombia was plagued by violence, especially in rural areas, where party loyalty was very fierce.

The war ravaged the cities too, however. For example, Jorge Eliécer Gaitán was murdered by an assassin on a street in Bogotá. Gaitán was a widely popular advocate for the working class and was beloved by his followers. In their grief over the loss of their leader and in response to years and years of social frustration, the people rioted and destroyed the city's downtown area. Two thousand people died in the rioting, which became known as "the Bogotazo."

The tensions that previously existed between Liberal and Conservative politicians soon spread to all Colombians fed up with social injustice, corruption, poverty, and a lack of authority. Rioting erupted throughout the country, especially in rural areas where there was the least amount of governmental control. Both Liberals and Conservatives and their respective supporters committed unspeakable atrocities against one another. In the town of Puerto Tejada on the Cauca River, for example, as described by David Bushnell, "Liberals murdered leading Conservatives, decapitated them and then played soccer in the main plaza with the severed heads."[16] Criminals used this period of mayhem to commit senseless acts of violence and banditry.

Finally, in 1953 there was a military coup. The leader of the coup, General Gustavo Rojas Pinilla, took over the government, proclaiming himself president. To get a hold on the violence, General Pinilla launched a campaign of all-out military repression. He curtailed civil rights, repealed pro-labor laws, forced labor unions to disband, censored the press, and challenged the freedom of worship. To control any opposition to himself, he decreed that if anyone spoke disrespectfully of the president they could be jailed or fined. To frighten the public into submitting to his rule he committed more and more brutal acts against even the slightest acts of opposition. For example, in 1956 at a political rally that became known as the

This 1957 photo shows Colombian police attacking student protesters in Bogotá with water cannons. General Gustavo Rojas Pinilla brutally suppressed all opposition to his government.

Bull Ring Massacre, those who did not cheer loud enough for him were killed or wounded. But after years of such tight control on the populations, Pinilla could not get the fighters to lay down their arms.

Over the many years of this war, thousands of refugees fled the countryside to the cities to escape the violence and to look for work. Unemployment, overcrowding, and poverty skyrocketed in all of Colombia's major cities. When the war ended in 1958 some 250,000 people had died. In Colombian history this horrible time would later be known simply as *la Violencia,* meaning "the Violence."

THE NATIONAL FRONT ERA

By 1957 most political groups opposed Pinilla. His dictatorship had almost destroyed democracy in Colombia. Although the two main parties rarely agreed on anything, they both saw that Pinilla was a dangerous man and that returning democracy to Colombia would require removing him from power.

To remove Pinilla, leaders from the two main parties joined forces and formed what they called the National Front. They signed a declaration to form a coalition government that would share power between the Conservative and Liberal parties for sixteen years. They also agreed to alternate the presidency between the two parties every four years. Pinilla did what he could to stop the formation of the National Front but was eventually forced into exile in Spain. Soon after, Colombians voted to approve the National Front and elected a new president, Lleras Camargo.

Although the National Front created a system to share power between the two parties, the system was far from democratic. The people did not choose which party they wanted in power because, as outlined in the National Front arrangement, if the last president was from the Liberal Party, the next president would automatically come from the Conservative Party. Furthermore, the two parties made it nearly impossible for people outside either party to gain any position of power. As a result, election after election usually returned the same people to power.

In addition to being undemocratic, the National Front had not solved Colombia's social and economic problems. Many Colombians still lived in poverty and had little access to schools, little or no health care, and scant opportunities to improve their lives. In addition, a sizable percentage of the population could find no way to enter the political process in order to enact laws that would alleviate their problems. Underground political groups who had grown impatient and frustrated began forming. These groups attracted the poor and unemployed who took up arms to make life better for themselves. Colombia was yet again on the brink of another bloody civil war.

Revolutionaries Challenge the Establishment

Several revolutionary groups were formed during the 1960s, each with the goal of improving the lot of Colombians. All of the groups fought for such changes as land reform, free education, free health care, and fairer distribution of wealth. Some of these groups aimed to transform Colombia's economic system from capitalism to communism. One group, the Ejército de Liberación Nacional (National Liberation Army or ELN), for example, hoped to bring about a Communist revolution similar to the one that had recently occurred in Cuba. In addition to the ELN, there were two other main revolutionary groups: the Fuerzas Armadas Revolucionarias de Colombia (Revolutionary Armed Forces of Colombia), more commonly known as FARC, and the Movimiento 19 de Abril (Nineteenth of April Movement), known as the M-19.

These revolutionary groups used ruthless tactics to achieve their goals. They brought on years of unrest and bloodshed and Colombia found itself in an almost constant state of war-

COLOMBIA'S GUERRILLA GROUPS

Colombia has been engaged in guerrilla warfare for forty years. Colombia's guerrillas are the oldest and largest insurgent forces in Latin America, with roots going back to *la Violencia*, which began in 1948. The original aim of these revolutionary groups was to transform the social order and to change the way Colombia was governed.

The largest group, FARC, was founded in 1964 by Communist peasants. Their leader, nicknamed "Tirofijo," meaning "sure-shot," wanted land reform and better working conditions for agricultural workers. By 2001 there were about eighteen thousand FARC members. To join the political process legitimately, they formed the Union Patriótica.

Another guerrilla group, the ELN, was created in 1965. It was inspired by a workers' revolt which was spreading throughout South America. ELN members were typically middle-class youth, but by 2001 it was estimated that the ELN had thirty-five hundred members from all walks of life.

A third major guerrilla group was born in 1973: the Movimiento 19 de Abril, or M-19, named in honor of the date when Rojas Pinilla lost the presidency. This day was a victory for them because they had opposed the former military dictator. This group was urban in origin and sought greater social equality. They eventually laid down their arms and became peaceful participants in the political process.

Over the many years of violence, these groups have secured for themselves fairly large, rural zones where they function as if they are legitimate authorities. As of 2003 the government of Colombia continues to try to disarm or destroy these guerrilla groups.

fare. The government forces were not equipped to battle this type of unconventional warfare, known as guerrilla warfare. Guerrilla warfare sometimes includes kidnapping citizens, attacking civilians, and ambushing public or private buildings.

During this time the United States began to focus on the problems of violence and poverty throughout Latin America, particularly Colombia. In 1961 the United States developed an aid program called the Alliance for Progress under which it loaned Colombia $732 million to enact land reforms; build homes, hospitals, and schools; and improve the country's transportation systems. Despite the aid, only ninety thousand of the more than four hundred thousand landless peasant families received land. Both illiteracy and unemployment increased, and almost two-thirds of rural Colombians continued to live in absolute poverty. The U.S. Senate's report on the program concluded, "Colombia had barely begun to tackle the problems of more equitable income distribution and the country's social structure remained essentially unchanged." [17]

Meanwhile armed conflict against the government continued. Over time, guerrilla fighters became part of prosperous

A large group of mourners attends the funeral of Carlos Pizarro, head of the M-19, one of several revolutionary groups that have been active in Colombia since the 1960s.

military enterprises. Combatants were paid to engage in warfare. With unemployment and poverty rampant, fighting for the revolutionaries was the only paycheck a person might be able to secure. The guerrillas established zones in isolated areas of the countryside beyond the control of government forces or any type of legitimate legal authorities. From these remote, well-armed encampments, they planned further attacks upon the government. The most tragic of these attacks occurred in 1985 when the M-19 seized the Palace of Justice in Bogotá. Government forces stormed the building and in the ensuing fight, the building exploded into flames. More than one hundred people died, including an estimated thirty guerrillas and eleven supreme court justices.

Throughout the ongoing years of guerrilla warfare against the government, civilians were often caught in the crossfire. In the countryside where there were few government authorities, the guerrillas controlled the peasants using brutal methods. They would seize their land, sometimes forcing farmers to switch from growing corn and yucca to growing coca, as coca brought in far more money. They would share little of the profits with the peasants. Those who complained or tried to oppose the guerrillas were killed or kidnapped. If local governmental authorities did not submit to guerrilla rule, they too were killed or kidnapped.

THE RISE OF THE DRUG WARS

To carry on fighting the guerrillas needed weapons, food, housing, and money. To raise the funds necessary to support themselves, they sold illegal drugs, especially cocaine. Cocaine quickly became a major, albeit illegal, export from Colombia. Much of the Colombian cocaine was sold illegally in the United States. To stop the illegal drug trade in both of their countries, the U.S. and Colombian governments began working together. They destroyed cocaine fields and processing factories in Colombia, intercepted planes and boats used to bring the drugs into the United States, and used American military forces to assist the Colombian military and police. But despite these efforts, the illegal drug industry and its associated violence continued.

With seemingly no end to the drug trade and little progress being made in the war against the government, a small but dedicated number of Colombian vigilantes formed paramilitaries—or organized groups of armed men—to destroy the guerrilla forces and their supporters. In 1987 there were, according to authors Frank Safford and Marco Palacios, "one hundred and forty self-defense groups dedicated to fighting guerrillas and their civilian sympathizers." [18] Unfortunately, the entry of yet more groups of combatants only increased the violence. Now, in addition to destroying the guerrilla forces, the government also had to contend with stopping the paramilitaries, which often committed atrocities against anyone they considered their enemy, guerrilla fighter or civilian. Some of the fighting had little to do with achieving solutions to social problems but were personal vendettas, village feuds, power struggles over control of the drug trade, and other outright criminal activities.

A Colombian antidrug force confiscates bricks of cocaine. Many rebel groups have turned to the illegal drug trade to help fund their operations against the government.

By the 1980s Colombia had one of the world's highest homicide rates, much of it due to warring criminals vying for control of the fast-growing, lucrative drug trade. Since much of the fighting occurred in rural areas, there was little government or police presence. Even if the authorities were able to control the fighting, they too took sides or took money to look the other way when crimes were committed. Making matters worse, Colombia's notoriously corrupt judicial system did little to punish criminals. Disrespect for the law thus became common. As years went by, using violence became a normal way to solve conflicts. Engaging in a violent lifestyle even came to be admired among many young men. To own guns, kill enemies, and to die fighting showed that a young man was tough, brave, and powerful.

A Century Ends; a New One Begins

By 1990 democracy in Colombia was under threat. Colombia's government was ridiculed and called a "narco-democracy" because its major institutions such as the police force, the judicial system, and government officials were involved with drug traffickers. In 1991 Colombia once again rewrote its constitution aiming to address these problems by making the government more democratic, encouraging new parties to develop, and improving human rights. The country was divided into thirty-two departments, each with its own capital under the authority of a popularly elected governor. In addition, this new constitution of 1991 eliminated any reference to Roman Catholicism as the religion of the nation. The new constitution put some new faces in government, and voter turnouts rose.

Despite the many challenges facing the nation, life was improving for many Colombians. For example, by 1993 about 80 percent of Colombian homes had electricity, although nearly two-thirds of the population still lacked drinkable water. But the war continued and its effects continued to plague the country. By 1998 rebel forces controlled nearly half of Colombia's territory. The people who lived in these areas were in constant fear as warfare between the paramilitaries, government forces, and guerrillas waged around them.

In 1998 a new president, Andrés Pastrana, initiated talks with the major guerrilla groups in the hope of establishing a lasting peace for Colombia. Pastrana knew the FARC wanted to overthrow the government and rule all of Colombia, but to start

the peace process he made a conciliatory gesture. He officially gave the FARC, who now numbered about sixteen hundred men and women, most of the area they had taken by force. The hope was that this offer of land would contain and appease them. The FARC now had complete control of an area in southern Colombia that was about as large in size as Switzerland.

Once the FARC was given the land, they agreed to talk with the government, but not to a cease-fire, so the violence continued. Talks continued on and off for almost three years. The government would not agree to FARC demands to try to curb the activities of the paramilitary forces. But in the interest of keeping the peace process moving forward they made some concessions to the guerrillas. For example, the government agreed to not punish the guerrillas for kidnapping people. Colombians, not surprisingly, were disappointed in this agreement, and it further eroded their faith in their government institutions.

Andrés Pastrana (center) became Colombia's president in 1998 and he implemented a short-lived peace agreement with the country's rebel groups.

By 2002 the peace negotiations broke down. It became clear to government negotiators that the FARC had no real intentions to make peace. Instead the FARC had used the time spent negotiating to maintain control over that newly acquired area. To regain the territory given to the FARC, government forces renewed their attacks against them. The FARC retaliated by exploding car bombs among civilian populations. The paramilitaries continued to fight the guerrillas and attack their alleged supporters. Colombia's violent conflict waged on with seemingly no end in sight.

SOLVING COLOMBIA'S PROBLEMS

In the beginning of the twenty-first century, Colombia remains a developing nation coping with an ongoing war, an illegal drug trade, and a host of social and economic problems. For example, Colombia's judicial system seems ineffective as convicted criminals often go unpunished. Unemployment in 2000 was 16 percent and crime rates are high.

Both Europe and the United States have loaned enormous sums of money to Colombia to help it solve its many problems. The primarily U.S.-funded antidrug, social welfare, and economic growth program of some $7.5 billion dollars is called Plan Colombia. It is too early to tell if Plan Colombia will succeed. The ongoing conflicts seem to be deeply rooted and severely threaten progress in this developing nation. However, whereas other Latin American countries fell into dictatorships during times of instability, Colombia has remained democratic throughout most of its history. This fact is a beacon of hope pointing the way to a brighter future for Colombians as this nation struggles to make life safer and more prosperous for its people.

Daily Life of Colombians

The many lifestyles of the people of Colombia reflect the great diversity of its geography. Despite modern communications and transportation, Colombians are divided by geography and tend to identify themselves by their regions. The greatest differences in lifestyle can be seen between those who have wealth and those who are poor. For example, some 14 percent of Colombians live on less than one dollar a day and about 55 percent of Colombians live below the poverty line. Comparatively, 12 percent of Americans live in poverty. Poor Colombians live in shacks without running water, are underfed, and some do not even own basic furniture. In contrast, wealthy Colombians often have several maids, cars, large homes, and the typical machines—computers, DVD players, cell phones, digital cameras—of middle- and upper-class Americans.

Colombians do have some characteristics in common. For instance, most Colombians—about 76 percent—are urbanites, living in or around the country's four main cities, Medellín, Cali, Bogotá, and Barranquilla. And almost all Colombians are Roman Catholics.

Religion and Family

The church is one of the most important mainstays of life in Colombia. Colombians are more loyal to the church than to any other Colombian institution. Colombians typically attend church to observe life's rites of passage, such as birth, marriage, and death. It is not uncommon for Colombians to make a pilgrimage at least once in their lifetime to a Catholic holy site, such as Cerro de Monserrate, a mountain overlooking Bogotá which has a church at its peak. The church is often the central organizing force in towns throughout Colombia. For example, Nancy Ramirez Botello, a homemaker from Bogotá currently living in the United States, explains, "In small towns in the Cundinamarca department the church organizes a system of sharing livestock among all the townspeople." [19]

The Catedral Primada de Colombia, Bogotá's largest church, dominates the city's main plaza. Roman Catholicism plays an integral part in daily Colombian life.

Catholic practices are followed in almost all schools, whether public or private. For instance, in most schools, teachings of the Catholic religion are part of the curriculum, as is daily prayer and the use of Catholic religious symbols such as paintings of saints and Jesus. Photographs of the pope and crosses are displayed throughout most schools. In addition, except in the most remote regions of the country, children usually participate in the rituals of the church, such as attending church services, while at school.

Roman Catholicism has long been an integral part of life in Colombia. Its rules, traditions, and practices were established centuries ago and despite modern influences, many Colombians continue to follow these rules. Since the days of conquest, the rules of how one should live were dictated by Catholicism. For example, since divorce is not permitted in

Catholicism, Colombians rarely divorce. In addition, children are expected to be baptized, given godparents, and raised to participate in the church's rites of passage. Since the latter half of the twentieth century, Catholicism has slowly become less important in Colombia. For example, in 1991 the Colombian constitution replaced references to "Sacred Heart of Jesus" with "God." In addition, today Protestantism is growing in Colombia, and Protestants are no longer outcasts.

These changes, however, have not affected the church's teachings on the sacredness of family, and thus Colombian daily life still revolves around the family. Families are incredibly important to Colombians. Although most Colombian families are not large—two or three children in a family—a household will often include grandparents, aunts, uncles, cousins, and other relatives. A Colombian family—no matter where family members live—forms the basis of all social and business relationships. As Colombian Nancy Ramirez Botello says, "Even when we live far away from each other, we stay close."[20] Family members often go to great lengths to support one another. For example, it is common for Colombians who emigrate to another country to send money to their families back home to help them out.

COLOMBIAN WAY OF LIFE

Besides tight-knit families, Colombians also share a preference for a slow pace of life. Throughout Colombia, whether in the slums of the city, the mansions of the rich, or the small and large farms throughout the countryside, Colombians live by a slower pace than most people of the United States. For example, on weekends Colombians gather with friends and family for long leisurely meals, rather than filling the time with many activities. Indeed, mealtimes are rarely quick snacks. For example, lunchtime, even on weekdays, is usually at least a one-hour meal for almost all Colombians. In general, there is little rushing about as being punctual is not considered important.

Another aspect of daily life that is familiar to almost all Colombians is making goods by hand. Author Gustavo Wilches-Chaux explains, "Despite the growth of modern industry and commerce, most goods and services in [Colombia] are still produced with traditional methods. A large percentage of the Colombian population continues earning its income in domestic and local craftshops."[21]

A Colombian man sips a cup of coffee at an outdoor café. Colombians regularly savor coffee in the company of friends and family.

Colombians also share a taste for similar foods. In general, Colombian meals show a mix of indigenous, African, and Spanish foods. As tropical fruits are abundant in Colombia, Colombians eat many different kinds of them, or make them into smoothies and drinks. One favorite is *maracuya,* a passion fruit that has a tart, pineapple-like flavor. Another popular fruit is the *lulo,* which looks like a cross between a peach and a lemon and tastes similar to a pineapple and mango. Some favorite Colombian foods are potatoes, rice, and a root called yucca. Vegetable and bean soups are very popular with most Colombians and are eaten sometimes at breakfast. Another food commonly eaten by Colombians is arepa, a grilled cornbread, sometimes filled with cheese.

Colombians also share a love of coffee, which is the country's traditional drink. Because Colombia has many regions ideal for growing coffee, it is widely available and served often. A particular favorite coffee drink is *tinto,* which is a very small cup of coffee with lots of sugar. Whenever coffee is served it is meant to be savored, especially in the company of friends and family.

DAY-TO-DAY FUN

Getting together with families and friends is probably Colombia's favorite pastime. People often get together on Sundays for visiting, and Saturday nights are popular for dancing and listening to music. Because most of Colombia is warm, many of these get-togethers occur outdoors. Not surprisingly, life in Colombia is noisy. As described by author Krzysztof Dydynski, "Music blares from restaurants, is pumped into buses . . . televisions are at full volume." [22]

Watching television is also a popular pastime. Since many Colombians do not own their own televisions, people gather in a bar or restaurant or at friends' and relatives' homes to watch television together. Colombians who are wealthy enough to own a television and a video player rent videos or DVDs. Popular shows in Colombia are called *telenovelas,* prime-time soap operas that tell dramatic stories full of passion. These *telenovelas* are broadcast as often as six nights a week. Each one lasts about six months. In the countryside where there may be few televisions, or none at all, people will gather around and listen to radio shows. Another popular pastime is watching soccer matches and bullfighting on television or at the stadiums and arenas.

Perhaps the most treasured pastime is simply relaxing. Colombians work very hard during the workweek. When they have free time Colombians love to simply be with one another, telling stories; sharing jokes; arguing about politics; discussing what is going on in their villages, towns, and cities; and enjoying their time off from work. The American tradition of doing many activities for entertainment is not common in Colombia. Most Colombians do not have enough leisure time nor a lot of money to spend for entertainment. For the most part, they use their free time merely to rest and be with their families.

THE WEALTHY IN COLOMBIA

Although everyone enjoys spending time with families and friends, wealthy Colombians occupy their leisure time quite differently than the poor. For fun they eat out in fine restaurants, travel outside the country, or attend cultural events. It is also common for middle- and upper-class families to spend time at exclusive, private social and sports clubs. These clubs, explains Agustín Diaz, a Colombian schoolteacher, "actually designate which class you belong to,"[23] so belonging to a club is more than just for fun. It is a way to show others one's status.

The middle and upper classes in Colombia also have at least one maid to do the family's sewing, laundry, cooking, cleaning, and food shopping. They also usually send their children to private schools. Their children attend colleges and universities, sometimes in other countries. These families usually work in professional circles, as cultural, educational, government, and business leaders. Although they account for less than 25 percent of the population in Colombia, they wield a great deal of power.

Among the wealthiest of this group are those who own many of the major industries of the country. It has been said that Colombian centers of power, such as industry, land ownership, and the government, belong to twenty-four family dynasties descended from the Spanish conquerors who have governed the country for more than one hundred years.

ETHNICITY IN COLOMBIA

It is not only wealth that determines who is powerful in Colombia. Ethnicity also defines one's social and economic opportunities. Afro-Colombians and Indians are still considered lowest on the social status ladder and find it very difficult to enter the spheres of power that control industry and politics, which are primarily controlled by mestizos and direct descendants of the Spaniards. These prejudices are, however, changing. For example, mestizos were once considered of a lower class than the descendants of the Spaniards. Today they are now fully integrated into the social and political life of Colombia.

However, discrimination against Afro-Colombians and Indians continues, not only because of their ethnicity, but also because they are less educated. Some 43 percent of Colombians, mostly Indians and Afro-Colombians, do not attend high school because they live in areas where there are no secondary schools or they must work to help support their families. Only 60 percent of Afro-Colombians, *zambos* (African-Indians), and Indians can read and write.

La Palanca: The Lever That Gets Whatever You Want

In Colombia, the words *la palanca* literally mean "the lever." And just as a lever opens something, *la palanca* in Colombia means opening an opportunity, or as Americans say, pulling strings. It can mean a favor, or a bribe, or using one's connections to get something, such as a job or entrance into a university. Sometimes *las palancas* are used to get something done by a government agency more quickly, such as getting a driver's license. Since *las palancas* usually involve trading favors between people, the more personal connections Colombians have with individuals of power or influence, the more easily they get what they need.

Mixing between ethnic groups is frowned upon in Colombia. Indians and Afro-Colombians usually do not marry one another. However, because mestizos' skin color can vary greatly, they intermarry with both Afro-Colombians or Colombians of purely Spanish ancestry. Colombians who consider themselves pure Spaniards usually socialize with and marry only others they also consider pure Spaniards and who have a last name that is familiar to them.

Although ethnicity can sometimes define one's social class in Colombia, Colombians also determine a person's class by his or her last name. Having an illustrious last name indicates that a family has a long history of living there and of being part of the inner circles of power. Although Colombians usually have at least two last names, one from one's mother and one from one's father, some people retain also their grandparents' names to show others that they are from important or purely Spanish families. Explains Elsa Borraro, a Colombian photographer, "My grandmother considered our family lineage very important so she taught me ten of our family's last names. Our names show how much white blood our family has. This was important to my grandmother." [24]

Indigenous Colombians

Most Colombians live in cities, but about 1 percent of the population, some five hundred thousand indigenous peoples, live far from urban areas of Colombia. Overall, there are about eighty of these indigenous groups, speaking some sixty

A Guambiano woman poses for a photo in traditional dress, including a black skirt, a derby-style hat, a shawl, and many strands of white beads around her neck.

different languages. Some of these indigenous peoples live in villages with only a hundred or so people, while other groups are much larger. Some groups remain completely isolated from other Colombians, such as the Motilón, who live high in the mountains in northern Colombia. This group is hostile to outsiders and even in recent times has attacked missionaries or oil company employees with poisoned arrows and blowguns (hollow reeds that one blows hard pellets through).

The largest group of natives are the Paéz and Guambiano, who number about fifty thousand and live in the southern highlands of Colombia. These groups have their own government of an annually elected council. They farm corn, beans, and yucca. They also raise turkeys and sheep. The women weave cotton and wool to make garments. Their homes are made of bamboo and the roofs are thatched.

Guambianos are most recognizable on market day, the one day of the week when everyone gathers in the nearest plaza to sell their wares. On this day both men and women wear handmade, traditional dress which includes a long black skirt with pink trimmings, flat or derby-style black or gray hats, and leather boots. The women also wear royal blue shawls with fuchsia fringe draped over their shoulders and many strands of white beads around their necks. The colors of their clothing represent their belief in the unity of all living things.

Another notable group of Indians are the Wayuu, who live on the Guajira Peninsula. Today many of the Wayuu work in the coal mines of El Correjón. Others, however, still live as

THE KOGI

The Kogi are an isolated indigenous group living in the higher regions of the Sierra Nevada de Santa Marta. They are very protective of their land and few outsiders, including Colombians, have visited them. Because their society has changed little in the past five centuries and they survived the invasion of the Spanish conquerors, they are considered unique.

The Kogi are primarily farmers, growing such crops as potatoes, beans, plantains, and sugarcane. They also raise oxen, pigs, sheep, chickens, and turkeys. They make hammocks, nets, bags, and ropes from the fibers of the agave plant. They weave their own fabric for clothes and make their own tools from wood and stone.

The Kogi have no written language, so their history and religion is passed down through stories told from one generation to the next. Their spiritual and social lives are led by male shamans called *mamas,* who are chosen at birth and spend the first nine years of their lives in a cave in total darkness learning about the spiritual world. After puberty they choose whether or not to return to the caves to continue their spiritual education. If they decide to become *mamas* they stay in the caves, returning to Kogi society when they are about twenty years old.

Despite their ancient ways, the Kogi are beginning to learn Spanish in their efforts to work with the Colombian government to protect their lands and their way of life. The Kogi are a cultural treasure unique to Colombia.

they have for hundreds of years, building temporary shelters for themselves made of cactus branches as they move with their cattle, sheep, and goats to find water and grazing land.

The way of life for the Wayuu is, however, changing. With the construction of paved roads to reach mines and the flow of money coming in from foreign sources, the Wayuu no longer are dependent on raising animals and bartering for all they need. More and more of the Wayuu work in the mines to earn money and now can buy modern goods. Thus the Wayuu's ancient way of living entirely off the land is slowly disappearing.

There are, however, some indigenous groups that still live as they have done for thousands of years. They have kept their ancient ways by shunning outsiders and the modern way of life. They go by their tribal names and do not consider themselves Colombian. Throughout the Chocó and Amazon regions these small groups of Indians are almost entirely dependent upon the resources of the forest. They do some farming, growing manioc (a root plant), corn, plantains (bananas), and peanuts. They hunt small wild animals, such as monkeys and tapirs, and almost any kind of bird. A local delicacy is ants fried in oil or fat. These Indians weave wild cotton for clothing and use nets, basket traps, and spears to catch fish in the rivers and streams that crisscross through their land. They travel these waterways in canoes made from hollowed-out trees.

THE CAMPESINO, OR COUNTRY PEASANT

There are also Colombians who live in the countryside, like the indigenous peoples, but unlike them, they do not shun outsiders and are part of mainstream Colombian life. Most of them are mestizos. They primarily work in the coffee, sugarcane, or other agricultural industries. Often families, including children, work together. Children go to school infrequently, or only for a few years when they are very young because they must work to help support the family. In addition, getting an education can be difficult because schools are far away and there are no buses to take children to school.

Rural people tend to live to according to the old customs and traditions that have been passed down from generation to generation. Their daily lives, therefore, in some ways are not modern. For example, rural people do not spend much time learning from books. In fact, it is not uncommon to find rural people who do not read or write. Their religious beliefs have also been passed down from the older generation; they mix Roman Catholic beliefs with ancient traditions and spiritual customs originally from indigenous peoples. For example, rural people often rely on chants or rituals to heal, rather than antibiotics and other modern medicines. Also, they are likely to believe that droughts, famines, and other such ordeals are punishments sent from evil spirits or an angry God.

But most importantly, rural life revolves around work. People in the countryside have a long day of work that includes not only farm work, but other household tasks such as cooking food without a lot of modern conveniences and making clothes. Without shops nearby, clothes cannot be bought, so families make their own clothes. They might not have running water, so children are often responsible for fetching water from a well nearby. Typically, a fire pit is used to cook and boil water. Children are usually responsible for collecting firewood to keep the fire going.

The day begins very early—at 4 A.M.—with a big breakfast that might include leftovers from the night before: arepas, bread, eggs, broth, and fruit. Breakfast always includes a cup of coffee sweetened with unprocessed, brown-colored sugar. At midmorning is another meal and then a large meal is eaten at midday when the workday is over. Before bed another light, simple meal consisting of rice and fried plantains, potatoes, meat, or fish is eaten.

The country peasant wears simple clothes and lives in a modest home. If a family is especially poor they might not own shoes. If the weather is cool, almost all country people wear a cloaklike garment called a ruana draped over their shoulders. This same garment might also be used as a blanket. A family's one-room home is made of slats of wood or pressed earth. The roof might be metal or thatched with grasses. Sometimes the floor is earthen. Usually the home is built on stilts to keep the house dry and away from dangerous biting snakes and insects. Indoor plumbing is rare. Water is instead pumped outside from a well. The toilet is usually outside in a small closet and the kitchen is usually in a shed attached to the home, often not enclosed on all sides. A family usually has few possessions, but almost every family owns a battery-operated radio to listen to music, weather reports, news, or talk shows.

Peasant work varies according to where a family lives. On the llanos, for example, taking care of cattle is the primary

The highlight of life for most rural Colombians is the weekly market day, when they travel to town plazas to sell their goods and visit with friends.

work available. On the Pacific coast a family might farm crops, pan creeks for gold, work in the mines, or work on banana or sugar plantations. For most families living in rural areas, people do whatever work is available, such as cutting wood, mining, farming, picking produce, cutting sugarcane, processing sugar, scavenging for emeralds in aboveground mines, or fishing. Most families own too little land—usually not quite three acres—to grow extra food to sell, growing just barely enough to feed themselves.

The highlight of rural life is market day, which occurs once a week. People travel from great distances to sell clothing, woven fabric, small animals, food, and craft items. They visit with one another and shop for food in the village store. If one is feeling sick, market day is the time to seek out help from a witch doctor or shaman. "In every market place worthy of its salt," writes author Gustavo Wilches-Chaux, "there is an . . .

Indian selling curative herbs, spangle [shiny] necklaces, armadillo shells, love incantations [spells], and amulets [a magical object] against bad spells." [25]

THE COFFEE INDUSTRY

The crop that provides the most work for the largest number of Colombian peasants is the coffee bush. Throughout the western regions of the country, concentrated especially around the city of Manizales in the western mountains, about four hundred thousand men grow, harvest, and process coffee on many small to medium size properties. The *cafetero,* or coffee industry worker, learns his trade from his father and usually attends an agricultural school. To harvest coffee, workers stand on very steep slopes, usually for about ten hours a day, and pick ripe coffee fruit. After the beans are picked they are spread out to dry in the sun or dried in ovens. When they are dry, the beans

A farmer picks coffee beans on a farm near Bogotá. Harvesting coffee provides work for hundreds of thousands of Colombians.

LADDER BUSES

Many people do not own cars in Colombia, and there are few railroads connecting the villages, towns, and cities. To get around, Colombians, especially those who live in the countryside, use buses. Some of these buses are called *chivas* or ladder buses because of the ladders on the sides that are used to climb up to the top of the bus.

These buses do not stop at designated bus stops but whenever people need to get on and off. They usually move along very slowly, and are often jam-packed. If there is no room inside, a passenger can sit up on the roof of the bus. To get off, a passenger flags the driver or calls out to stop the bus.

Author Krzysztof Dydynski, in *Colombia: Where the Amazon, Andes and Caribbean Meet,* describes a typical *chiva:*

> The *chiva* is a piece of popular art on wheels. The body is made almost entirely of wood and has wooden benches, rather than seats. . . . The body of the bus is painted with colorful decorative patterns, each different, with a main painting on the back. *Chivas* take both passengers and any kind of cargo, animals included.

> Decorations might also include religious icons, or plastic statues, pictures of famous soccer players, singers, or other notable Colombians. The *chiva* is truly a unique Colombian form of transportation.

Many rural Colombians get around on chivas, *open-air buses with colorfully decorated wooden bodies.*

are further processed and then packaged for shipping to all parts of the world.

Colombians living in the coffee-growing regions are usually better off than those who live in the forests or plains, as coffee has usually been a profitable crop. Some even own their own coffee farms. Because these workers are better off, their homes are usually made of more substantial materials, such as brick or stone, than those of peasants. Their children go to school more regularly and for more years. Families typically have access to medical care, and they usually have enough to eat. But like all country people throughout Colombia, they work very hard and own little.

LIFE IN THE CITY

Life in the city is very different from life in the country. There are enormous differences between the lifestyles of the rich and poor that can be seen from neighborhood to neighborhood within a short distance from each other. Life is comfortable and easy for wealthy city dwellers as they have many household goods and conveniences, such as indoor heating and air-conditioning, washing machines, televisions, computers, cell phones, and cars. Overall, middle- and upper-class urbanites who are well off live a lifestyle that looks similar to that of people in the United States, although it is only the very wealthy who own luxury cars and many televisions, computers, and telephones in one household.

Middle- and upper-class Colombians tend to wear fine clothing, designer jeans, or custom, hand-tailored clothes. In fact, it is common for well-to-do Colombians in the city to have their own seamstress or tailor make their clothes. Middle- and upper-class Colombians in the city eat out in fine restaurants or fast-food restaurants such as Burger King and Pizza Hut. They drink many of the same things as Americans, such as espresso, capuccino, or other coffee drinks and soda. They shop in supermarkets where they choose from a great selection of both domestic and imported foods. Middle- and upper-class Colombians in the cities work at jobs similar to Americans in manufacturing or service industries.

For the poor in Colombian cities, life is very different from that of the well-off. Even food is less plentiful and life is a daily struggle. They live in hillside slums called *tugurios.* They often have had little formal education. They have little access to medical care, a low rate of literacy, and few opportunities to improve their lot in life. Children whose families cannot care for them end up living on the streets, begging and stealing food to survive. Their parents are often unemployed and work only sporadically, finding odd jobs or collecting cans or bottles to sell.

Whether rich or poor, all Colombians have had to learn how to cope with living with violence. Wealthy Colombians hire bodyguards and travel in armored cars. The poor simply do not go out much. Everyone avoids troublesome neighborhoods and the countryside. Because Colombians have adjusted their lifestyles to avoid violence for decades, these habits have become commonplace. People do not dash about in fear and it is not constantly on their minds that they live in a violent country. Like other nations that cope with violence, Colombians have learned to appreciate what is special about their country, such as their strong traditions, their religion, and close-knit families. Despite their hardships, Colombians are not embittered or fearful. They are known for being easygoing and joyful. As Shakira, one of their famous pop singers, once declared, "We Colombians never forget how to smile." [26]

CREATIVITY WITH A PASSION: ARTS AND CULTURE

The diversity found in Colombia's people has created variety in their arts and reflects their many sources of inspiration and traditions, from the earliest pre-Hispanic civilizations to trends that are found throughout the world today. Geography has also contributed to the diversity of art in Colombia. Separated by obstacles such as mountains, swamps, and rivers, particular regions developed certain kinds of art forms. For example, Colombia's Caribbean seacoast developed unique cultural traditions in dance that only recently have spread throughout the country. Bogotá on the other hand, is best known for its literature. However, all of the arts of Colombia show the influence of the indigenous, African, and Spanish cultures. Most recently, Colombians have developed an appreciation of their indigenous artistic heritage from the early civilizations. Today this heritage is the basis for many modern Colombian art forms.

FESTIVALS AND HOLIDAYS

Colombians enjoy many festivals—a festival of some kind is usually happening somewhere in the country celebrating everything from local historical events to nationwide religious holidays. There are some two hundred festivals every year. Some of the most popular celebrations are the country's many regional beauty competitions. Authors Raymond Leslie Williams and Kevin G. Guerrieri note that "there is a crowning of a new beauty queen in Colombia on an average of once a week." [27] Most of Colombia's many festivals and celebrations are religious, though, and have been celebrated for several centuries. For example, every village and town has its own Catholic patron saint and a day to honor that saint. Typically the celebration includes religious ceremonies, parades, and feasting.

The country's national holidays include religious occasions such as Christmas and Easter. Christmas in Colombia is celebrated more modestly than the many other Christian holidays that are celebrated. For example, children in Colombia typically do not get toys for Christmas. Instead, Colombian children often get clothes to welcome in the new year that follows Christmas.

One of the most important national religious holidays in Colombia is Carnaval, or "carnival," which occurs in February or March. This celebration is in preparation for the upcoming season of sacrifice, or Lent, and includes indulging in all types of vices, such as overeating or drinking too much liquor. The country's most elaborate celebration of Carnaval takes place in the Caribbean coastal city of Barranquilla. The Carnaval of Barranquilla is a wild four-day fiesta that has been celebrated for centuries in Colombia. When the festival begins, all normal city life ceases as the streets come alive with costumed dancers, nonstop loud music, parades, continuous outdoor parties, and masquerades. A parade of floats covered with flowers streams down the main streets. Thousands of people dress up in fancy clothes and costumes and also go on parade. According to author Krzysztof Dydynski, "Carnaval de Barranquilla is probably the most colorful . . . of all Colombia's festivals."[28]

The other major religious festival is Semana Santa, or "Holy Week." This is the most important Roman Catholic religious celebration, not only in Colombia, but throughout South America. The most elaborate festivities of Holy Week are held in the cities of Popayán in the southwest and Mompós in the north. Many Colombians come to these two cities from all over the country to celebrate Holy Week. Each city has elaborate evening processions in which statues of the city's saints are paraded through the streets. Numerous religious services are held in churches, religious retreats are conducted, and biblical events are publicly reenacted. The week's events conclude with Easter Sunday, a day filled with church services, more religious processions, and holy music.

Colombia also celebrates many sporting events, such as the Feria Taurina, the international bullfighting season that occurs throughout the country in January and February. During this time there are bullfights every Thursday and Sunday in the larger cities throughout the country. Other sporting celebrations are strictly local, such as the unusual Torneo de Coleo, or "Tournament of the Tail," held in the town of Villa Vicencio around Christmastime. In this event cowboys on horseback attempt to flip over a bull or cow by the tail.

One of the most unusual festivals in Colombia is the Carnaval de Blancos y Negros, or the "Carnival of the Black Ones and White Ones," celebrated in the small southern city of Pasto every January 5 and 6. The origins of this event go back to the days of Spanish rule when slaves were permitted to hold a celebration. To show their approval for the festivities the slave masters painted their own faces black. On the following day, slaves painted their faces white. So on January 5, Día de los Negros, or "Day of the Black Ones," all the people

Most Colombians engage in indulgent behavior during Carnaval in anticipation of the long season of sacrifice known as Lent.

A man wears face paint and a colorful hat in celebration of the "Carnival of the Black Ones and White Ones," a two-day celebration that occurs every January in the southern city of Pasto.

paint or dust their own faces with grease or ashes. On January 6, Día de los Blancos, or "Day of the White Ones," all the people paint their faces with chalk or flour. According to the day, those with unmarked faces get chased down and get their faces painted black or plastered white by the celebrants.

MUSIC OF COLOMBIA

Whether a solemn church service or lively street festival, music is a significant part of any celebration in Colombia. Music has always been an important part of religious ceremonies, festivities, and battles. Before the arrival of the Spaniards, indigenous peoples typically used wind and percussion instruments. The Africans and Spaniards brought with them drums, guitars, accordions, different kinds of flutes, and many other kinds of instruments to make music. A distinctive Colombian style evolved that mixed music from Spanish, indigenous, and African cultures. Although all kinds of music are played and enjoyed throughout the country, each region of Colombia has its own special kind of music: for example, *joropos* are folk songs that originated from the eastern plains near the Venezuelan border. Other popular styles of music, such as *cumbia* and *vallenato,* come from the Caribbean coastal region.

Typical instruments used in Colombian music are the *flauta,* an Indian flute; the *tiple,* a guitarlike instrument; and the *raspa,* a percussive instrument made from a gourd and played like a washboard. But just as rhythms come from different regions, the instruments used also vary from region to region. For example, along the Pacific Coast many types of African percussive instruments are used. In the Andean regions, guitars and other stringed instruments—which are Spanish in origin—are more typically used. The music of the plains is usually accompanied by a harp, a four-stringed guitarlike instrument called a *cuatro,* and maracas, which are rattle-like instruments.

One of the many traditional instruments used in Colombian music is the cuatro, *a small guitarlike instrument.*

COLOMBIA'S NOBEL LAUREATE: GABRIEL GARCÍA MÁRQUEZ

Although there are many fine Colombian writers, Gabriel García Márquez is the country's only writer to have received international acclaim. In fact, he won the Nobel Prize in Literature in 1982. Many of his works have been translated into many other languages and he is considered one of Latin America's greatest writers. He has written novels, film scripts, essays, and articles.

Márquez was born in 1928 in the small Colombian town of Aracataca. He began his writing career as a journalist and reporter for local newspapers, later moving on to become a foreign correspondent in Europe and New York. Márquez's career took off after the publication in 1967 of *One Hundred Years of Solitude*, a novel that was a best-seller worldwide. It tells the story of a family that lived for many generations in a small town in Colombia.

Colombian Gabriel García Márquez is one of the world's most celebrated writers.

COLOMBIAN DANCES

Another favorite art form in Colombia is dancing. As with music, dances are regional in origin. For example, the dances of *bambuco, guabina,* and the *torbellino* are from the interior highlands. *Cumbia, mapalé,* and *bullerengue* dances are from the Caribbean coast. *Cumbia,* a dance with African origins, is Colombia's most famous dance. This dance's name comes from the West African word *kumb,* meaning "noise and celebration." The music of this dance combines an African beat, made by using hand drums, flutes, and whistles of Indian origin, with Spanish verse. As with most dances, although originally from one area, the *cumbia* is now danced throughout Colombia.

The dances of Colombia usually have different purposes. Some dances such as the *cumbia* tell a story, usually of courtship and love between a man and a woman. Some dances such as the *torbellino,* which is intended to mimic the movements of a whirlwind, create the illusion of natural occurrences. Other dances such as the *bullerengue,* which is African in origin, are ritualistic. The *bullerengue* is an initiation dance that celebrates puberty in young girls. Some dances such as the *currulao,* which comes from the Cauca region in southwest Colombia, are so wild and sexual in their movements that they have been banned several times throughout Colombia's history.

THE LITERATURE OF COLOMBIA

Dancing and music are Colombia's favorite artistic forms, but other arts, such as the literary arts, have always been held in high regard as well. According to the *Economist,* "Colombia's cities are teeming with bookshops, and its exports of books exceed those of any other Latin American country."[29] Several of Colombia's statesmen, such as Simon Bolívar, Camilo Torres, Antonio Nariño, and Francisco de Paula Santander were all talented writers. According to authors Raymond Leslie Williams and Kevin G. Guerrieri, "Writing has been viewed as a higher calling [and can serve] as a passport into politics, diplomacy, or the cultural bureaucracy."[30]

Poetry in particular is perhaps Colombia's most beloved literary form. There is a Colombian saying that for every one hundred inhabitants, Colombia has two hundred poets. Indeed, the country has had many poets of acclaim throughout its history. Rafael Núñez, one of Colombia's most famous romantic poets, served as president of Colombia four times in his life.

Colombian novelists are widely read throughout Colombia. One of the nation's most renowned writers was Jorge Issac, a poet and novelist. His most famous book, *María,* although written in 1867, is still read today. It is an example of a classic novel that uses the style of writing called Latin American romanticism, which deals with love, patriotism, nature, and religion. In more recent times the most widely acclaimed Colombian writers have been the poet Germán Pardó García, novelist and poet Alvaro Mutis, and novelist Gabriel García Márquez, winner of the Nobel Prize in Literature in 1982. Márquez, considered Latin America's greatest writer, created a new style of writing, which critics call "magic realism," that uses a mixture of myths, dreams, and reality. Many writers have copied this style and it is now known worldwide as a particular literary form.

FINE ARTS AND CRAFTS OF COLOMBIA

Colombians are also known for their fine arts and crafts, especially basketry, pottery, leather, and woven goods. Some regions are particularly noted for certain crafts. For example, the woven handbags from the Arhuaco tribe are prized for their exceptional beauty and high quality. And the people of Mompós, a town southeast of Cartagena, make handworked gold filigree jewelry and rocking chairs reputed to be the best quality nationwide. Craft workers are also notable in Colombia because many still use ancient patterns and styles, such as the *mola,* a rectangular cloth with colored designs, and ruanas, woolen ponchos made in the colder regions of the Andean zone. Rudimentary hand looms used many centuries ago are still used by Colombian artisans in many regions today.

Colombian artists have earned national and international acclaim. During the 1950s and 1960s Alejandro Obregón was considered the most influential painter in Colombia. His paintings often depict Colombian flora and fauna. Rodrigo Arenas Betancur, a widely recognized sculptor, is known for his monumental public works that typically include patriotic and social messages. Internationally, Fernando Botero is currently Colombia's most acclaimed living fine artist. His sculptures and paintings are recognizable by the largeness of his figures. Botero's work is an excellent example of the unique quality of Colombian art wherein European classical traditions are combined with the folk styles of Colombia. Today

Botero's paintings and sculptures are shown in museums, public squares, and parks throughout the world.

SPORTS IN COLOMBIA

Sports are yet another important part of cultural life in Colombia. *Fútbol,* or soccer, is Colombia's favorite sport. Colombians will stop doing just about anything to watch their soccer team on television. Stadiums are filled to capacity when there is a soccer game in town. Soccer is also a very popular sport to play and outstanding professional soccer players are admired throughout the country.

A player from the Colombian national team heads the ball during a World Cup soccer match. Soccer is Colombia's favorite sport.

Other popular sports are bicycling and race-car driving. Colombia has produced several world champion cyclists and has enjoyed success at world-class racing events. Colombian Juan Pablo Montoya, for example, is a Formula One team driver. In 2001 he received the Ibero-American Community Trophy that is given each year to the most eminent Latin American sports person.

Finally, one of the most popular sports is *tejo,* or *turmequé,* an indigenous game played throughout the country. Almost every Colombian town has a *tejo* court to play this game, which is similar to horseshoe pitching. The object of the game is to throw the *tejo,* a smooth round piece of metal or stone, and hit the target that contains a small amount of gunpowder that explodes on impact. Whether it is enjoying an afternoon's game of *tejo* with neighbors, dancing the *cumbia* in a festival, or listening to a *vallenato,* Colombians love to partake in the arts.

CHALLENGES FACING COLOMBIA

With its vast endowment of marketable resources, Colombia could provide well for its people. In fact, Colombia has a healthier economy than many of its neighboring countries. However, the country is mired in several economic problems that inhibit wide-scale prosperity. In addition, the guerrilla war continues, as does an illegal drug trade, environmental degradation, violations of human rights, high unemployment, widespread poverty, and general violent lawlessness. Until these problems are worked out, Colombia will remain a troubled nation.

CITIZENS UNDER ATTACK

The violence that plagues Colombia is affecting civilians in alarming numbers. Guerrilla warfare has occurred in 66 percent of all municipalities in Colombia. In the election for mayors in 2003, at least twenty-five candidates were killed and eight others kidnapped. To control this lawlessness the country's current president, Álvaro Uribe, has increased the police presence throughout the country and launched a program to arm peasants, but violence continues.

Of greatest concern to Colombians from all walks of life is the threat of kidnapping, which has proved to be a profitable method for guerrillas and other illegal armed groups to raise funds for their operations. Since 1998 an average of about three thousand people a year have been abducted, mostly by the FARC and the ELN. Ordinary citizens as well as congressmen, politicians—even a former presidential candidate—have been kidnapped. Some of those who have been kidnapped are held for years. According to government figures, some twenty-five hundred to four thousand people were being held in 2003.

Another threat to Colombians is forced disappearances—taking people away and not returning them—often committed

VOICES OF KIDNAPPING

Voices of Kidnapping is a radio show that was created in 1994 by Herbin Hoyos, a radio journalist who had at one time been kidnapped. While Hoyos was held hostage, he and a fellow inmate listened eagerly to the radio for news about themselves, but there was none. Eventually Hoyos escaped from his captors. When Hoyos returned to his job he wanted to do something to help those who are kidnapped to know they have not been forgotten. He therefore developed a radio broadcast that would give hope to Colombians who have been kidnapped and those who await their return.

Voices of Kidnapping airs every Sunday morning sending messages of love from families anxiously awaiting the fate of their brothers, fathers, mothers, or sisters who have been kidnapped. Callers get one minute of air time to send their message of love to those who have been kidnapped, with the hope that their message will be heard. For the estimated three thousand people currently being held hostage, if they hear these messages, it is a glimmer of hope. For their friends and families, a message sent is their only chance to reach out to their loved ones.

The radio show Voices of Kidnapping *allows parents like these to send messages of hope to their loved ones who have been kidnapped by guerrillas.*

by the Autodefensas Unidas de Colombia (AUC), a right-wing terrorist group. No ransom is asked for these people, and most likely they are killed. Sometimes they are taken because the AUC does not like their political views or their associates, but they may be taken for any number of reasons.

Forced disappearances and kidnappings are not the only things that endanger the lives of Colombians. Colombia has one of the highest murder rates in the world. In 2002 there were seventy-eight murders per one hundred thousand people, some eleven times higher than in the United States. There are several reasons Colombia has such a high murder rate. One reason is Colombia's history and culture. In the past, it was not uncommon to kill someone for revenge, to preserve one's honor, or resolve personal conflicts. This tradition continues today.

The most recent cause of murder is the illegal drug trade. Since the drug trade is so lucrative, drug dealers and their fellow criminals often kill one another to control the trade in particular areas. But most important, murder is widespread in Colombia because murderers usually receive only a mild punishment. According to the *Economist,* "Murderers . . . can expect to serve an average of only four-and-a-half years in jail."[31] It is also difficult for the authorities to control this particular crime because Colombians are too fearful for their own lives to report a murder they may witness. A common saying in Colombia is *por ver caer,* which means "to see is to die."

A NATION AT WAR

Colombia's other main cause of violence is the war, which has claimed the lives of tens of thousands of civilians and combatants over the past five decades. Nearly thirty-five hundred people are killed a year. According to a U.S. Senate report an average of 2.8 bombs goes off every day in Colombia. President Uribe has promised to expand the government's military forces in order to destroy the guerrillas and paramilitaries. But destroying these armies will not be easy, especially since the FARC and the ELN joined forces in 2003. Their forces currently number about twenty-five thousand.

However, some successes against the FARC were achieved in 2002, when some forty-six thousand FARC guerrillas were captured. But capturing guerrillas is not enough. The reasons for joining the guerrilla forces—to escape poverty and unemployment—remain. And Colombians, especially young men and women, continue to join the guerrillas and fight against the government they blame for not solving the country's problems.

Indeed, war has become so deeply entrenched in the lives of some Colombians that they cannot imagine *not* being at war. As quoted in the *Chicago Tribune,* Humberto, a thirty-nine-year-old former police officer who receives a salary of two hundred dollars per month as a guerrilla fighter claims, "I like war. It's where I feel most comfortable." [32] Guerrilla fighters enjoy their occupation because it provides them with a decent salary and they can then provide for their families. Poor Colombians, even children, are thus likely to join the guerrilla forces just to earn a wage. "There is a lot of hunger," explains Victor Estrada, a Colombian coffee farmer and priest. "Kids without work will take whatever is offered to them, including joining the armed groups." [33]

PEACE WITH THE PARAMILITARIES

Although no peace agreement has been reached with the two main guerrilla groups, President Uribe has made progress in demobilizing the AUC, a terrorist group with an estimated twenty thousand members. In July 2003 the AUC agreed to a cease-fire and plans to be completely disarmed by 2005. This accord has restored some of the public's confidence in the government's ability to bring an end to Colombia's decades-long war. In addition, it is hoped that disarming the AUC will lessen the overall violence in Colombia as the AUC has been blamed for the greatest number of killings and forced disappearances in Colombia since 1995. It is also expected that there will be a reduction in the illegal drug trade since the AUC finances its operations with drug trafficking.

POVERTY IN COLOMBIA

The warring factions have also created a great deal of poverty. Every day thousands of Colombians flee from their homes and communities to escape the violence. Since 1985 the war has displaced about 2 to 3 million people, representing the third largest internal refugee crisis in the world. In 2002 alone, some 410,000 people were displaced by the war. Since most of the warfare takes place in the countryside, the majority of the

displaced are rural peasants. Many of the displaced people have little or no formal education and therefore have few ways to make a new life for themselves when they leave their communities. Without their land, they cannot support themselves.

Another reason for rural poverty is the lack of suitable farming land. Centuries ago the best land was owned by a small number of families who kept it in their families generation to generation. It has been a very lengthy and sometimes violent process to force these large landowners to sell or share land with the peasants who have actually worked it. Some government administrations have forced landowners to sell

FARC guerrillas make their way through the jungle. The ongoing war between guerrilla groups, paramilitary forces, and the government is the biggest threat to Colombia's prosperity.

Many families like this one in the high Andes live in areas without available farmland. Some families resort to illegally clearing unsettled plots in order to farm them.

or give portions of their properties to the poor. Other administrations have done just the opposite and returned land to wealthy landowners. The poverty of Colombian peasants usually persists because no effective land reform is ever enacted.

To remedy their situation, some peasants have attempted their own land reform. They have illegally cleared and settled some 8.5 million previously unsettled acres, or about one-quarter of the nation's territory, which they do not own. These remote regions, however, are also attractive hideouts for narcotics traffickers and guerrilla fighters. Unfortunately for the peasants, wherever the guerrillas go, paramilitaries and government forces follow and bring their war with them. Whenever the violence comes too close to their homes, the peasants move on again, searching for even more remote regions to try to live in peace.

OBSTACLES TO PROSPERITY

Finding a peaceful place to live is just one challenge facing rural Colombians. Prosperity is even more elusive. There are some 10 million Colombians who live in poverty and will probably stay poor for many reasons. First, because they have little say in the political process they can do little to pass laws

CHILD PEACEMAKERS

In 1996 the children of Apartuadó, a town torn apart by guerrilla fighting, formed their own children's government to advocate for peace. They wrote stories, poems, and letters and painted pictures describing their experiences of living in a war zone. They drew up a "Declaration of the Children of Apartuadó," stating, as quoted in the Web site PeaceNews, "We ask the warring factions for peace in our homes, for them not to make orphans of children, to allow us to play freely in the streets and for no harm to come to our small brothers and sisters . . . we ask for these things so our own children do not suffer as we have done."

The children of Apartuadó held peace carnivals to bring together feuding communities and learned how to counsel children displaced by violence. They also attended a nationwide peace workshop organized by UNICEF. At the workshop, representatives of children from throughout Colombia organized a special election known as the Children's Mandate for Peace and Rights. In 1998, 1999, and 2000 their movement was even nominated for a Nobel Peace Prize. These children have worked hard to make the world aware of their situation, and dream of a peaceful Colombia.

that might improve their situations, such as ensuring free or affordable health care for their families. Second, they cannot move upward in class because Colombian society is highly rigid. Third, they cannot improve their situations because their daily lives are consumed with such problems as getting clean water or finding a doctor. For example, in rural areas 30 percent of the population does not have access to clean water and there is only one physician per thousand people. (As a comparison, there are almost three physicians per thousand people in the United States.)

Finally, the most serious obstacle to finding prosperity is the lack of job training for the poor. They are not learning how to use the new technologies and therefore cannot work at better-paying jobs. For example, most Colombians do not have computers or Internet access. Only about 4 percent of Colombians use personal computers. As of 2001, whereas 50 percent of all Americans were Internet users, in Colombia only 3 percent of the people used the Internet. In addition, finding well-paying jobs is next to impossible for poor Colombians because they are not well educated. Although primary schooling is free, an estimated 20 percent of urban children and 40 percent of rural children do not attend school. Only about half of Colombian children ages fifteen to eighteen are in school full time. As a comparison, in the United States, 80 percent of this age group attend school. In rural areas, schools might only offer education for the first five primary grades. Without education and technical skills, peasants must continue doing the lowest-paying work available, such as farming, manual labor, household work, making handicrafts, or very simple factory work.

About half of Colombians work in what is called the informal sector of the economy, meaning they pay no taxes. This means they also receive no benefits, such as social security. Thus, when they lose their jobs, or get too old to work, or get injured or sick, they simply cannot earn any money. Since there is no social safety net to help Colombians who work in the informal sector, without work they quickly fall into dire poverty.

Colombia does very little to help the poor, but there are some social service programs. For example, the Social Support Network, which is scheduled to operate through 2006, offers help to about 1.8 million severely poor Colombians living in rural areas. They receive job training, internships, and help keeping their kids in school. This program also includes jobs paying $117 a month—a typical minimum wage in Colombia—for digging ditches, hauling dirt, and laying roads. However, this program only helps a small fraction of the people in dire need.

With all the obstacles facing the poor in Colombia, some turn to trading in illegal drugs, fueling yet another problem that this nation struggles with today—its illegal drug industry. As quoted in the November 27, 2001, *Dallas Morning News,* Colombian economist Roberto Steiner states, "Poverty and lack of economic opportunity are the top factors contributing to the decision of farmers . . . to abandon their legal livelihoods and join the underworld of the drug trade."[34]

ILLEGAL DRUGS

Colombia has become the world's leading supplier of cocaine, supplying about 70 percent of the world's cocaine and about 90 percent of the cocaine that is sold in the United States. This country is also one of the major players in the worldwide drug trade of heroin. The drug trade has been highly profitable for a select few. In fact, drug traffickers in Colombia have become so wealthy that, as writers Raymond Leslie Williams and Kevin G. Guerrieri explain,

> They have had considerable influence in virtually all spheres of Colombian life. Drug money [has] penetrated everything, from the ownership of professional athletic teams to the sponsorship of beauty queens in national pageants. Even the campaign and presidency of a former president, Ernesto Samper, who served from 1994 to 1998, was tainted by overwhelming evidence that he had received drug money during his campaign.[35]

Drug traffickers have even given substantial funds to social service causes, such as building schools and affordable housing.

Drug kingpin Pablo Escobar greatly profited from Colombia's illegal narcotics trade.

Colombia has received about $2.5 billion from the United States to combat the drug trade. This includes supplying equipment to spray herbicides on coca fields to kill the plants. Funds are also sent to train the Colombian police and army in counternarcotics operations. The funds to combat the drug trade have also been spent creating other jobs for former coca farmers. For example, five thousand former coca producers now work as forest rangers. Their job is to watch over those areas where coca plants have been destroyed so that they will remain free from coca or poppy cultivation. International agencies agree with the government's assertions that, as of 2003, these efforts have cut poppy production between 25 and 40 percent and coca production by a third—although the drug trade is far from being eliminated entirely.

It is hoped that a decrease in drug trade will help Colombia end its long-standing war. In 2003 President Uribe said, "In the absence of drugs, we can defeat terrorists [guerrillas] easily." [36] Since the guerrilla groups fund a good deal of their operations through the drug trade, halting the trade is key to hampering their war against the government. However, it is too soon to tell if either the drug trade or guerrilla violence can truly be stamped out.

THE MANY USES OF THE ANCIENT PLANT COCA

The coca plant is used to make cocaine, a highly dangerous, addictive, and illegal drug. Trade in this plant, specifically its derivative, cocaine, has brought violence and disorder to the countryside and upheaval and corruption in the government of Colombia for many years.

Before cocaine became a popular drug in Europe and the United States, indigenous groups in Colombia used the coca leaf for thousands of years to increase energy, reduce hunger and thirst, and as a part of religious ceremonies. The use of cocaine for entertainment purposes is not part of their culture. Colombian Indians in the past and still today make a mixture of the coca leaf and ash, which they keep in a pear-shaped squash and carry in a shoulder bag. By licking the coca mixture from a wooden straw, they can undertake long hunting journeys or travel to faraway markets without stopping to eat or sleep.

THE ENVIRONMENT AND ILLEGAL DRUGS

President Uribe's current programs to eradicate coca and poppy fields by spraying them with herbicides are strongly supported by the government of the United States and some Colombians. But opponents, such as human rights groups, environmentalists, and farmers, claim that spraying poses significant health and environmental risks.

Growing coca itself poses major risks to the environment. Rain forests are cleared to make room to grow coca. In fact, in the Andean region, coca cultivation has destroyed almost 6 million acres of rain forest—an area larger than the states of Maryland and Massachusetts combined. These ecologically unique forest habitats are valuable because they support rare and endangered species of animals and plants. If there is no rain forest, the plants and animals cannot thrive. Drug traffickers also destroy rain forest when they build landing strips for planes that are used to ship the cocaine from Colombia to Europe, the United States, and elsewhere. They also cut down rain forests to build laboratories to process the raw coca and poppy into cocaine and heroin. Additional damage to the environment is caused when the laboratories dump toxic chemical waste, thereby poisoning nearby plants, rivers, and soil.

Environmental problems are also posed by the spraying programs. Environmentalists claim that the chemical sprays kill not only the coca but also other plants, birds, mammals, and aquatic life, especially in the Amazon region. Linda Farley, a scientist at the American Birds Conservancy, says, "The long term, indirect ecological effects [of the spraying] are severe."[37] Also, spraying does not necessarily mean a farmer will stop growing coca. In fact, spraying sometimes only causes some farmers to clear more rain forest to replant coca. Despite the dangers of growing an illegal crop and the resulting environmental damage, cocaine will continue to be a more profitable crop than the traditional Colombian crops of corn and yucca so long as there is a demand for it.

"LAWS WILL GIVE YOU FREEDOM"

In the twenty-first century, despite ongoing violence, more and more Colombians are surviving infancy, getting enough to eat, getting an education, and living longer. More and more Colombians can get medical care. But years of violence have tainted this nation, forcing enormous amounts of energy and resources to be spent trying to end the civil war.

Colombia continues to be a nation divided into dozens of zones of power, where the rule of law is not what is written in the country's constitution but is decided by whoever is most powerful. And this domination is usually achieved through violent means. Compounding the violence is that Colombia still lacks, as it always has, a strong, well-respected, centralized authority to maintain peace from border to border. To achieve peace Colombia must contend with the many citizens who have serious grievances and long-standing anger toward their government.

Colombia's challenges in the twenty-first century are many. But if the government makes significant progress toward ending the war and providing better opportunities for its people, then the riches of this beautiful country can be truly shared by all Colombians. To bring about lasting peace Colombians have only to follow their highest ideals as written above the doors of their Palace of Justice in Bogotá: "Colombians, arms have given you independence, laws will give you freedom."

FACTS ABOUT COLOMBIA

GOVERNMENT

Full name: Republic of Colombia

Capital: Bogotá; population 6,422,198 (2003)

Government type: republic

Administrative divisions: thirty-two departments

President: Álvaro Uribe (since May 2002)

Independence: July 20, 1810

Elections: chief of state and vice president elected for four-year term; senate, 102 seats, and house of representatives, 106 seats elected by popular vote to serve four-year terms

Cabinet: coalition of two dominant parties and independents

GEOGRAPHY

Area: 440,700 square miles

Bordering countries: Panama, Venezuela, Ecuador, Brazil, Peru

Climate: tropical along coast and eastern plains, cooler in highlands; ranges from forty-five to seventy-five degrees Fahrenheit

Terrain: flat coastal lowlands, central highlands, high Andes mountains, eastern lowland plains

Elevation extremes: Low: Pacific Ocean: 0 feet; High: Pico Cristóbal Colón and nearby Pico Simon Bolívar, both at 18,947 feet

Natural resources: petroleum, natural gas, coal, iron ore, nickel, gold, copper, emeralds, hydropower

Natural hazards: volcanic eruptions, earthquakes, droughts

Environmental issues: deforestation, soil and water quality damage from overuse of pesticides, air pollution in Bogotá

PEOPLE

Population (est. 2003): 44.2 million

Population growth rate (2003): 1.56

Birth rate (est. 2002): 21.59 births/1,000 population

Death rate (est. 2002): 5.66 deaths/1,000 population

Infant mortality rate (2003): 19 deaths/1,000 live births

Ethnic groups (2002): mestizo, 50 percent; white, 20 percent; mulatto, 14 percent; black, 4 percent; mixed black-Amerindian, 3 percent; Amerindian, 1 percent

Official language: Spanish

Literacy rate (2001): (over age 15) 92 percent

Life expectancy (2003): female, 75 years; male, 69 years

Religion (2003): Roman Catholic, 80–90 percent; remainder Protestant, Jewish, tribal, nonreligious

ECONOMY

Gross domestic product (2003): U.S. $268 billion

GDP growth rate (first trimester 2003): 3.81%

GDP per capita (2002): U.S. $1,947.9

GDP composition by sector (2001): agriculture, forestry, fishing: 13%; industry: 30%; services: 57%

Average annual income (2001): U.S. $1,890

Population below poverty line (2001): 55%

Inflation rate (2003): 7.2%

Monetary unit: peso; Colombian pesos per U.S. dollar—2,504

Labor force: 20.8 million (2003)

Unemployment rate: 14.8%

Chief products: textiles, coffee, oil, narcotics, sugarcane, food processing, emeralds, clothing and footwear, beverages, chemicals, cement, gold, coal, coffee, cut flowers, bananas, rice, tobacco, corn, cocoa beans, oilseed, vegetables, forest products, shrimp

Chief exports: petroleum, coffee, coal, gold, bananas, cut flowers, chemicals, emeralds, cotton products, sugar, livestock

Export partners: United States, Venezuela, Ecuador, Peru, Germany

NOTES

INTRODUCTION: TURMOIL IN A LAND OF BEAUTY

1. Quoted in *Economist,* "Colombia Survey," April 21, 2001, p. 5.
2. Gabriel García Márquez, *One Hundred Years of Solitude.* New York: Avon Books, 1970, p. 228.

CHAPTER 1: LAND OF MANY TREASURES

3. Frank Safford and Marco Palacios, *Colombia: Fragmented Land, Divided Society.* New York: Oxford University Press, 2002, p. 3.

CHAPTER 2: LAND OF MANY CULTURES

4. Quoted in Marc Lessard, *Colombia.* Montreal, Canada: Ulysses Travel, 1999, p. 28.
5. John Hemming, *The Search for El Dorado.* London: Michael Joseph, 1978, p. 51.
6. Lessard, *Colombia,* p. 15.
7. Safford and Palacios, *Colombia: Fragmented Land, Divided Society,* p. 60.
8. Safford and Palacios, *Colombia: Fragmented Land, Divided Society,* p. 56.
9. Jesús María Henao and Gerardo Arrubla, *History of Colombia,* ed. and trans. J. Fred Rippy. New York: Greenwood, 1938, p. 162.
10. Henao and Arrubla, *History of Colombia,* p. 329.

CHAPTER 3: A DIVIDED NATION

11. Quoted in U.S. Library of Congress Federal Research Division, "The Epic of Independence," http://countrystudies.us.
12. David Bushnell, *The Making of Modern Colombia.* Berkeley: University of California Press, 1993, p. 78.

13. Lessard, *Colombia,* p. 30.

14. Harvey E. Kline, *Colombia: Portrait of Unity and Diversity.* Boulder, CO: Westview, 1983, p. 38.

15. Quoted in Bushnell, *The Making of Modern Colombia,* p. 185.

16. Bushnell, *The Making of Modern Colombia,* p. 202.

17. Quoted in Gary MacEoin and Editors of Time-Life Books, *Colombia and Venezuela and the Guianas.* New York: Time-Life Books, 1965, p. 90.

18. Safford and Palacios, *Colombia: Fragmented Land, Divided Society,* p. 366.

Chapter 4: Daily Life of Colombians

19. Nancy Ramirez Botello, interview by author, September 16, 2003.

20. Botello, interview.

21. Gustavo Wilches-Chaux, *The Life of Colombia,* trans. Departamento de Lenguas Modernas de la Universidad Javeriana. Bogotá, Colombia: Villegas Editores, 1994, p. 31.

22. Krzysztof Dydynski, *Colombia: Where the Amazon, Andes and Caribbean Meet,* 3rd ed. Oakland, CA: Lonely Planet, 2003, p. 32.

23. Agustín Diaz, interview by author, September 17, 2003.

24. Elsa Borraro, interview by author, June 9, 2003.

25. Wilches-Chaux, *The Life of Colombia,* p. 168.

26. Quoted in Colombia Rocks, "The Stories: Shakira, the First Colombian to Win a Grammy Award," www.mibstarcom/colombia.

Chapter 5: Creativity with a Passion: Arts and Culture

27. Raymond Leslie Williams and Kevin G. Guerrieri, *Culture and Customs of Colombia.* Westport, CT: Greenwood, 1999, p. 29.

28. Dydynski, *Colombia: Where the Amazon, Andes and Caribbean Meet,* p. 144.

29. *Economist,* "Drugs, War and Democracy," April 21, 2001, p. 1.

30. Williams and Guerrieri, *Culture and Customs of Colombia,* p. 79.

CHAPTER 6: CHALLENGES FACING COLOMBIA

31. *Economist,* "Drugs, War and Democracy," p. 6.

32. *Chicago Tribune,* "Colombia Militia Scoffs at Peace: Militia Leader Has No Plans to Give Up," May 8, 2003.

33. *Chicago Tribune,* "Plunging Coffee Prices Fuel Coca Production, Civil War in Colombia," April 25, 2003.

34. *Dallas Morning News,* "Drug Cash Keeps Poor Farmers Afloat," November 27, 2001.

35. Williams and Guerrieri, *Culture and Customs of Colombia,* p 41.

36. Quoted in Ray Suarez, *OnLine NewsHour,* PBS, "Colombia's Struggle," October 6, 2003. www.pbs.org/newshour/bb/latin_america/july-dec03/colombia_10-06.html.

37. Quoted in Environmental News Network, "War on Drugs Takes Toll on Colombia's Environment, Farmers," March 21, 2001. www.enn.com.

CHRONOLOGY

3000 B.C.
Settlements of Tayrona, Caribs, Arawaks, Muisca, Sinú, San Agustin civilization, Quimbayá, Motilónes, Tumaco, and others are scattered throughout what is present-day Colombia.

A.D. 1499
Alonso de Ojeda lands on Guajira Peninsula.

1509–1520
Spanish colonize the area of Nueva Granada, or New Granada (modern Colombia, Ecuador, Panama, Venezuela).

1514
First bishop, Fray Juan de Quevedo, arrives.

1525
Santa Marta founded.

1533
Cartagena founded.

1538
Jiménez de Quesada founds Santa Fé de Bogotá.

1539
Nikolaus Federmann and Sebastián de Belalcázar arrive in Sante Fé de Bogotá.

1542
New laws enacted by Spain to stop slavery of indigenous peoples, among other provisions.

1550
Royal decree from Spain orders the suspension of all conquests, expeditions, and exploration.

1556
Church of San Francisco built in Bogotá.

1564
Audiencia (ruling body) of Santa Fé de Bogotá founded.

1571
First convent founded in Colombia (in Tunja).

1592
Spanish crown establishes reservations for indigenous peoples.

1599
Tayrona stage final rebellion against the Spanish.

1717
Viceroyalty of Santa Fé del Nuevo Reino de Granada separated from Peru.

1781
Comunero Revolt erupts.

1783
Use of Indian Chibcha language banned.

1814
Antioquia frees slaves in this region.

1815–1816
Reconquest by Spain quells rebellion.

1819
Simon Bolívar defeats Spanish at Battle of Boyocá.

1821
Gran Colombia created; children of slaves granted freedom.

1825
Slave trade abolished.

1831
Gran Colombia dissolves into New Granada.

1849
Conservative and Liberal parties formed.

1851
Male slaves and former slaves given full rights of citizenship.

1863
Republic of New Granada becomes Colombia.

1886
Republic of Colombia formed.

1899–1902
Civil war: Approximately one hundred thousand die in War of a Thousand Days.

1903
Panama declares independence.

1948–1957
La Violencia begins with the assassination of Jorge Eliécer Gaitán; approximately 250,000 die.

1953–1957
General Gustavo Rojas Pinilla establishes military dictatorship.

1957
Women get the vote.

1957–1973
Conservatives and Liberals form the National Front.

1964
Fuerzas Armadas Revolucionarias de Colombia (FARC) founded.

1965
Ejército de Liberacion Nacional (ELN) founded.

1985
M-19 takes over Bogotá's Palacio de Justicia (Palace of Justice). Nevado del Ruiz, a volcano in the central mountain region, erupts, killing twenty-five thousand.

1991
New constitution written.

1993
Pablo Escobar killed.

1997
Autodefensas Unidas de Colombia (AUC) founded.

1998

FARC is given forty-two thousand square kilometers of territory.

2002

Álvaro Uribe is elected president. Government reclaims FARC's territory.

2003

Cease-fire agreement reached between government and the AUC.

GLOSSARY

cacao: Cocoa bean.

campesino: Peasant, farmer.

centralist: An advocate of a form of government that has a centralized unit of power.

coalition government: A government which comprises multiple parties.

conquistador: Conqueror.

department: State.

disenfranchised: To be deprived of a legal right or privilege.

federalist: An advocate of a form of government that shares power between territorial units.

guerrilla: An armed fighter not part of government military forces.

indigenous: Native.

land reform: Distributing land equitably. Also called agrarian reform.

llanos: Plains.

mestizo: Person of Spanish and Indian ancestry.

paramilitary: Private army.

republic: A government where power resides in citizens entitled to vote.

shamans: Spiritual leaders or practitioners of spiritual processes.

traditionalism: Adherence to an inherited pattern of thought or action.

For Further Reading

Books

Sara Cameron in cooperation with UNICEF, *Out of War: True Stories from the Front Lines of the Children's Movement for Peace in Colombia.* New York: Scholastic, 2001. True stories of teens who have experienced violence and are involved in the Children's Movement for Peace in Colombia.

Lyll Becerra De Jenkins, *Celebrating the Hero.* New York: Lodestar Books, 1993. This novel is about an American teenager with Colombian roots. Enjoyable read that takes the reader into Colombia and Colombian family life.

Jill DuBois and Leslie Jermyn, *Colombia: Cultures of the World.* 2nd ed. New York: Marshall Cavendish, 2002. Simple text and many photos make this book an easy way to learn about Colombia.

Benjamin Villegas Jimenez, Gustavo Wilches-Chaux, and Benjamin Villegas, eds., *Colombia from the Air.* New York: St. Martin's, 1997. Beautiful aerial photographs of the landscapes of Colombia. Text primarily about the geography of the country.

Sarita Kendall, *Ransom for a River Dolphin.* Minneapolis, MN: Lerner, 1993. Set in the Amazon River region, this is an engaging story of children helping a wounded dolphin regain its health and spirit.

Marion Morrison, *Colombia.* New York: Childrens, 1999. Easy-to-read, well-illustrated, informative book about Colombia.

Web Sites

About.com (http://gosouthamerica.about.com/cs/colombia). Travel related. Good information about festivals, holidays.

Children of the Andes (www.children-of-the-andes.org/Colombia2.html). Great place to start learning about Colombia.

Has links to all the Web sites that have basic as well as specialized information.

Colombia: Contact Management Services (http://home1. gte/net/gomezedg/index.htm). All kinds of information about Colombia. Lots of pictures.

Colombia for Kids (www.travel-net.com/~embcolot/kids. html). Written especially for kids. Basic information, lots of pictures.

Embassy of Colombia–Washington, D.C. (www.colombia emb.org). Quick facts, travel and tourism information, and special interest topics.

Galeria Cano (www.galeriacano.com.co). Beautiful photos, great information on ancient cultures.

The Other Look of Colombia (www.theotherlookofcolombia. com). Web site has lots of popular culture information about Colombians, recent news from Colombia.

PeaceNews (www.peacenews.info). Reports on peace movements throughout the world.

The World Factbook: United States Central Intelligence Agency (www.cia.gov/cia/publications/factbook/geos/co.html). General information, history, up-to-date statistics.

Works Consulted

Books

Thomas Blossom, *Nariño: Hero of Colombian Independence.* Tucson: University of Arizona Press, 1967. Well-written, highly detailed biography of an important leader in Colombia's fight for independence.

David Bushnell, *The Making of Modern Colombia.* Berkeley: University of California Press, 1993. The definitive book for anyone doing research on Colombia.

Krzysztof Dydynski, *Colombia: Where the Amazon, Andes and Caribbean Meet.* 3rd ed. Oakland, CA: Lonely Planet, 2003. Summary of history, culture, arts of Colombia. Includes latest facts and figures.

John Hemming, *The Search for El Dorado.* London: Michael Joseph, 1978. Enjoyable read that details the European adventurers who first came to South America.

Jesús María Henao and Gerardo Arrubla, *History of Colombia.* Ed. and trans. Fred Rippy. New York: Greenwood, 1938. Language from another era makes it difficult reading, but worth it for the incredible details from firsthand accounts of historical events, documents, and people.

Harvey E. Kline, *Colombia: Portrait of Unity and Diversity.* Boulder, CO: Westview, 1983. Easy-to-read summaries of major events in Colombian history.

Armand J. Labbé, *Colombia Before Colombia: The People, Culture, and Ceramic Art of Prehistoric Colombia.* New York: Rizzoli International, 1986. Beautiful photos accompany short sections describing the crafts, legends, culture, and myths of preconquest peoples of Colombia.

Marc Lessard, *Colombia.* Montreal, Canada: Ulysses Travel, 1999. Extensive section on history does an excellent job of summarizing Colombia's past while including fascinating anecdotes not found elsewhere.

Gary MacEoin and Editors of Time-life Books, *Colombia and Venezuela and the Guianas.* New York: Time-Life Books, 1965. Pictures are dated, but do provide some idea of life in Colombia in the 1950s and 1960s.

Gabriel García Márquez, *One Hundred Years of Solitude.* New York: Avon Books, 1970. Best-selling historical novel that tells the story of a family living in a small town in Colombia.

Jorge P. Osterling, *Democracy in Colombia: Clientelist Politics and Guerrilla Warfare.* New Brunswick, NJ: Transaction, 1989. Scholarly work on very specific topic. Excellent examination of political process in Colombia.

John Leddy Phelan, *The People and the King: The Comunero Revolution in Colombia, 1781.* Madison: University of Wisconsin Press, 1978. Detailed, scholarly work on the Comunero Revolution.

Frank Safford and Marco Palacios, *Columbia: Fragmented Land, Divided Society.* New York: Oxford University Press, 2002. Thorough, scholarly work on the history of Colombia, especially its economic history.

Gustavo Wilches-Chaux, *The Life of Colombia.* Trans. Departamento de Lenguas Modernas de la Universidad Javeriana. Bogotá, Colombia: Villegas Editores, 1994. Beautiful photos and poetic text.

Raymond Leslie Williams and Kevin G. Guerrieri, *Culture and Customs of Colombia.* Westport, CT: Greenwood, 1999. Useful for learning about past culture and customs of Colombia.

PERIODICALS

Kathryn Arango, "Traditions and Innovations in Colombia," *Ceramics Monthly,* February 2003.

Chicago Tribune, "Colombian Militia Scoffs at Peace: Militia Leader Has No Plans to Give Up," May 8, 2003.

———, "Plunging Coffee Prices Fuel Coca Production, Civil War in Colombia," April 25, 2003.

Dallas Morning News, "Drug Cash Keeps Poor Farmers Afloat," November 27, 2001.

Economist, "Colombia Survey," April 21, 2001.

————, "Drugs, War and Democracy," April 21, 2001.

Juan Forero, "Colombia's Long Civil War Spreads Turmoil to Venezuela," *New York Times,* June 1, 2003.

Washington Post, "Uribe Sets Goal at Own Peril," September 20, 2003.

INTERNET SOURCES

Colombia Rocks, "The Stories: Shakira, the First Colombian to Win a Grammy Award," www.mibstar.com/colombia.

Environmental News Network, "War on Drugs Takes Toll on Colombia's Environment, Farmers," March 21, 2001. www.enn.com.

Claire Marshall, "The Cost of Kidnap in Colombia," *BBC News World Edition,* October 11, 2003. http://news.bbc.co.uk/1/hi/world/americas/3181586.stm.

Jeremy McDermott, "Colombia Hails Drug Crop Drop," *BBC News,* September 18, 2003. http://news.bbc.co.uk/1/hi/world/americas/3118644.stm.

Michele Norris, "Crop-Dusting Aids Colombia's War on Drugs," *All Things Considered,* National Public Radio, August 4, 2003. http://discover.npr.org/features/feature.jhtml?wfId=1385018.

Ray Suarez, "Colombia's Struggle," *OnLine NewsHour,* PBS, October 6, 2003. www.pbs.org/newshour/bb/latin_america/july-dec03/colombia_10-06.html.

U.S. Department of State, "United States Policy Towards Colombia and Other Issues," February 3, 2003. www.state.gov.

U.S. Library of Congress Federal Research Division, "The Epic of Independence," http://countrystudies.us.

INDEX

PICTURE CREDITS

ABOUT THE AUTHOR

Peg Lopata is a freelance writer and mother of two children. She has a bachelor's degree in sociology and master's degree in library and information science. She currently lives in New Hampshire.